MEDICARE
TURNING 65 IN 2025
OR RETIRING AFTER 65

   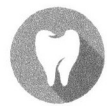  

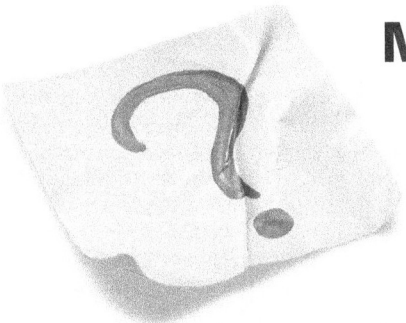

MOST COMMON MEDICARE QUESTIONS ANSWERED

CHRISTINE AMES
A 20-YEAR INDUSTRY VETERAN

© Copyright 2025 by Christine Ames and Christine Ames, LLC

Medicare: Turning 65 in 2025
Or Retiring After 65
Most Common Medicare Questions Answered

© Copyright 2025 by Christine Ames and Christine Ames, LLC
All Rights Reserved

No part of this book may be reproduced or transmitted in any form or by any means, electronic or mechanical, including photocopying, recording, or by any other information storage or retrieval system, without written permission from the author. The contents of this book may not be reproduced, duplicated or transmitted without direct written permission from the author.

Under no circumstances will any legal responsibility or blame be held against the publisher for any reparation, damages, or monetary loss due to the information herein, either directly or indirectly.

Legal Notice:
This book is copyright protected. This is only for personal use. You cannot amend, distribute, sell, use, quote or paraphrase any part or the content within this book without the consent of the author.

Disclaimer Notice:
The information presented in this book is meant to be used for general resource purposes only; it is not intended as specific financial advice for any individual and should not substitute financial advice from a finance professional. Appropriate decisions and actions depend on the exact circumstances, supporting facts, and regional interpretations, so the advice and strategies in this book may not be appropriate for individual situations. Please contact Social Security, Medicare, the specific insurance plan issuers, or other appropriate individuals or agencies for further guidance. Please note the information contained within this document is for educational purposes only. Every attempt has been made to provide accurate, up to date and reliable complete information. No warranties of any kind are expressed or implied. Readers acknowledge that the author is not engaging in the rendering of legal, financial, medical or professional advice. The content of this book has been derived from various sources. Please consult a licensed professional before attempting any techniques outlined in this book.
By reading this document, the reader agrees that under no circumstances is the author responsible for any losses, direct or indirect, which are incurred as a result of the use of information contained within this document, including, but not limited to, —errors, omissions, or inaccuracies.

The author disclaim any responsibility for positions or actions taken by individuals in reliance on the contents herein and shall not be liable for any damages.

ISBN: 979-8-9988930-2-5 (paperback)
ISBN: 979-8-9988930-3-2 (e-book)

CONTENTS

Introduction 1

Chapter 1: Is Medicare Free? 3
- Medicare Basics: Part A, B, C, and D.

Chapter 2: I Am Still Working and Turning 65 19
- Questions for Human Resources
- What to do if questions are answered
- Actionable Worksheet to Navigate Choices

Chapter 3: How Can I Avoid Medicare Penalties and Creditable Coverage? 35
- What is Creditable Coverage
- What Penalties to Avoid

Chapter 4: How to Enroll in Medicare 49
- Online
- Phone
- In Person

Chapter 5: Inflation Reduction Act 59
- Insulin Price Cap
- Elimination of the "Dounut Hole"
- Max Out of Pocket for Meds
- Changes to 2026 Plans

Chapter 6: Traditional Medicare / The Cadillac Plan . 71
- Traditional Medicare with a Medicare Supplement
- Which Plan is Best and Why
- Prescription Drug Coverage

Chapter 7: Medicare Advantage Pros and Cons . . 91
- Key Features
- Plan Types
- Networks, Medications, and Hospitals

Chapter 8: Common Rookie Mistakes 105
- Call Centers
- Food Card
- Give Back Plans
- ACA Plans
- Part D Plans

Chapter 9: Turning 65 and Open Enrollment 119
- Open Enrollment / Initial Election Period
- Guaranteed Issue
- Delayed Part B Enrollment

Chapter 10: Annual Enrollment and Other Election Periods. 131
- AEP or Annual Election Period
- OEP or Open Enrollment Period
- SEP or Special Election Period

Epilogue 143

INTRODUCTION

If you're turning 65 in 2025 and feeling overwhelmed by all the Medicare information flying your way—you're not alone. The mailbox is stuffed with brochures. The phone won't stop ringing. Your email inbox might be getting flooded too. Everyone has something to say, and yet none of it seems to match up. It's confusing, frustrating, and—if we're being honest—it can feel like way too much.

That's exactly why I wrote this book.

My name is Christine Ames and have worked in this industry for over 20 years. I've had the same conversation thousands of times. I've sat down with people who were still working, others who had already retired, and many who didn't even know if they were supposed to do anything at all. Some were worried about penalties and confused between group benefits and Medicare. Others didn't know the difference between Part A, B, C, or D. Almost everyone felt unsure of what came next.

I don't believe this process needs to be complicated. And I definitely don't think it should be scary.

That's why this book is different. It's not a sales pitch. It's not a gimmick. It's just real answers, explained in a way that actually makes sense. You'll find examples that mirror real-life situations, a step-by-step flow that follows logical order, and even a worksheet to help you make clear decisions about employer benefits. We've pulled from the most trusted sources—Medicare.gov, CMS, and the Social

Security Administration—so you're not just getting opinions. You're getting facts.

This book was written with *you* in mind. Let us talk plainly and keep it simple. Whether you're a planner who likes to get ahead or someone who's just starting to think about Medicare, my goal is to give you confidence, clarity and education.

You don't have to figure this all out alone. My hope is that this guide helps you feel a little less overwhelmed—and maybe even a little more empowered—as you prepare for what's next.

Let's simplify Medicare together.

CHAPTER 1

Is Medicare Free?

One of the first questions people ask when researching Medicare is whether it is free. Unfortunately, it is not free, although you have been paying your Medicare Tax for decades. While Medicare provides essential health coverage for millions of Americans, costs may be associated with each part of the program, depending on your income level. These costs help to fund the many services and areas of coverage that you enjoy as part of Medicare.

In this chapter, we'll break down the different parts of Medicare, looking at hospital insurance, doctor's insurance, and drug coverage. We'll also cover the income-related monthly adjustment amount (IRMAA) and if it applies to you and your spouse. We'll break down this often complex insurance system so you can understand what you need, what it entails, and what it might cost you.

By the end of this chapter, you'll understand what you have to pay, what each part covers, and if you may have to pay more due to your income. First, let's explore hospital insurance, also known as Part A of Medicare.

PART A: HOSPITAL INSURANCE, WHAT IT COVERS, AND WHAT IT COSTS

The first part of Medicare, or Part A, is most commonly known as hospital insurance. Hospital insurance is essential for inpatient care in hospitals, skilled nursing facilities, hospice care, and home health care. It is often one of the most affordable parts of Medicare because people usually don't have to pay a monthly premium.

One requirement for paying zero premium for Part A is that you or your spouse have paid their Medicare Care Tax for 40 quarters, which is equal to 10 years. In rare cases, some may have to pay a premium for Part A of Medicare.

With Part A of Medicare, a few different services are covered. From inpatient hospital care to home health care, here's what Part A covers and what to expect.

Inpatient Hospital Care

Inpatient hospital care refers to the care you receive when you are formally admitted to a hospital by a doctor. If you've gone in for surgery or spent a few days in the hospital, then you've experienced this already. Part A of Medicare covers the following:

- Hospitalization
- Skilled Nursing Care
- Blood
- Hospice Care

Part A Hospitals

SERVICES	MEDICARE PAYS

Hospitalization* Semi-private room and board, general nursing, and miscellaneous services and supplies
 	
• First 60 days
• 61st through 90th day
• 91st day and after:
  ○ while using 60 lifetime reserve days
  ○ once lifetime reserve days are used, additional 365 days
  ○ beyond the additional 365 days
	
	All but $1,676
	All but $419 per day
	
	All but $838 per day
	$0
	
	$0

Skilled Nursing Facility Care* You must meet Medicare's requirements, including having been in a hospital for at least 3 days and entering a Medicare-approved facility within 30 days after leaving the hospital • First 20 days • 21st through 100th day • 101st day and after	 All approved amounts All but $209.50 per day $0
Blood • First 3 pints • Additional amounts	 $0 100%
Hospice Care You must meet Medicare's requirements, including a doctor's certification of terminal illness	All but very limited copayment/ coinsurance for outpatient drugs and inpatient respite care

Adapted from Medicare.gov © Christine Ames LLC

Medicare was never meant to cover everything, and hospital stays are no exception. Just look at the chart—when you're admitted, you'll owe a $1,676 deductible upfront. Stay past 60 days, and suddenly you're paying $419 per day. Use up your 60 lifetime reserve days? That jumps to $838 per day—after that, Medicare covers nothing. Skilled nursing care? Medicare covers the first 20 days, but from day 21-100, you'll owe $209.50 per day—and after that, you're on your own. Need blood? The first three pints aren't covered. Hospice care is covered, but you may still have small copays for medications and respite care. As you can see, Medicare has gaps, and if you don't plan ahead, those gaps can get expensive fast.

Skilled Nursing Facility Care

If you require specialized medical attention and rehabilitation services after a hospital stay, it will be covered by Part A of Medicare. Skilled nursing facility care is something that many seniors require for a variety of conditions. This typically includes:

- Physical therapy (e.g., learning how to walk after surgery)
- Occupational therapy (e.g., relearning daily tasks after a stroke)
- Would care or IV medication that requires medical supervision
- Assistance with basic needs during recovery, such as bathing and dressing

Skilled nursing care is not the same as long-term care or custodial care, which is for a more extended period of time. The first twenty days of your stay at the skilled nursing care facility are provided at no cost to you. After 20 days, a recommendation will be made. This usually means receiving home health care, but some may move into a nursing home.

Hospice Care

For individuals with a terminal illness who are expected to live six months or less, hospice care is needed. This is covered under Part A of Medicare. Hospice is focused on comfort and quality of life rather than curing the illness. This type of care can include:

- Pain management and symptom relief
- Emotional and spiritual support for both the patient and their family
- Medical equipment (e.g., a hospital bed at home)
- Counseling and bereavement support for loved ones

Hospice care is available at home for no additional cost. However, hospice care in a facility charges room and board, which must be paid for.

Part A & B Home Health Care

SERVICES	MEDICARE PAYS
Home Health Care Medicare-Approved Services	
• Medically-necessary skilled care services and medical supplies	100%
• Durable medical equipment	
◦ First $257 of Medicare-approved amounts*	$0
◦ Remainder of Medicare-approved amounts	80%

Adapted from Medicare.gov © Christine Ames LLC

Home Health Care

Finally, the last type of care technically covered by both Parts A and B of Medicare is home health care. This is prescribed by your doctor if you need medical services at home, either after a hospital stay or because you cannot leave your home due to health issues. Covered services may include:

- Skilled nursing care (e.g., checking blood pressure or administering medications)
- Physical or occupational therapy
- Speech-language therapy
- Assistance with medical equipment or monitoring (e.g., oxygen machines or glucose monitors)

Unlike the other forms of care explained in this section,

home health care is generally short-term and meant to help someone recover or manage a condition without needing to be in a facility. Short-term care does not include long-term care that requires custodial care or memory care, which would be an additional cost out-of-pocket.

PART B: DOCTORS INSURANCE, WHAT IT COVERS, AND WHAT IT COSTS

Part B, or doctor's insurance, is paid by everyone or by the state through Medicaid. The premium is paid monthly and usually increases annually due to several factors. However, if you are in a lower income bracket, you may qualify to have some of your Part B premium paid for by Medicaid, meaning that it may be of little or no cost to you every month.

Medicaid income requirements vary from state to state, and there are multiple levels that you may qualify for. To get a clear answer of your specific costs based on your location and income level, please contact your local Medicaid office to make an appointment and application.

As of 2025, the monthly payment is $185 per individual. In 2024, individuals paid $174.70 per month; in 2023, it was only $164.90. However, some people may pay more due to income-related monthly adjustment amounts or IRMAA rules. We will cover this in a later section.

Part B of Medicare covers medical expenses both in and out of the hospital and outpatient hospital treatment.

These expenses or services include physician's services, inpatient and outpatient medical and surgical services and supplies, physical and speech therapy, diagnostic tests, and durable medical equipment.

- Examples of services covered under Part B of Medicare:
- Doctor visits with PCP or Specialist
- Surgery
- Blood Work
- MRI/CAT Scan
- Occupational, Speech, or Physical Therapy
- Chemo or Radiation

This is not a comprehensive list, but it does give you an understanding of what is included in your Part B of Medicare. Many more services not listed here could apply to your health situation now and in the future and are covered by Part B.

Medicare Part B helps cover doctor visits, outpatient care, and medical equipment—but as you can see in the chart, it doesn't cover everything. First, you'll pay the $257 deductible out of pocket before Medicare kicks in. After that, Medicare covers 80%, leaving you responsible for 20% of the bill, with no cap on how high that can go. A simple $100 doctor visit? You owe $20—not bad. But a $200,000 surgery? That's $40,000 out of pocket. Ouch. If your doctor charges more than Medicare's approved rate, you could owe even more. The good news? Lab tests like bloodwork

Part B Doctors

SERVICES	MEDICARE PAYS
Medical Expenses - In or out of the hospital and outpatient hospital treatment such as physician's services, inpatient and outpatient medical and surgical services and supplies, physical and speech therapy, diagnostic tests, durable medical equipment • First $257 of Medicare-approved amounts* • Remainder of Medicare-approved amounts	 $0 Generally 80%
Part B Excess Charges (above Medicare-approved amounts)	$0
Blood • First 3 pints • Next $257 of Medicare-approved amounts* • Remainder of Medicare-approved amounts	 $0 $0 80%
Clinical Laboratory Services • Tests for diagnostic services	 100%

Adapted from Medicare.gov © Christine Ames LLC

are fully covered. Home health care? Medicare pays 100% if it's medically necessary, but if you need durable medical equipment—like a wheelchair or oxygen tank—Medicare only covers 80%, leaving you with 20% of the cost. As you can see, these expenses can add up fast, so planning ahead is key.

PART C: MEDICARE ADVANTAGE, WHAT IT COVERS, AND WHAT IT COSTS

To enroll in Part C or Medicare Advantage, you must have both Part A and B Medicare.

Medicare Advantage, or Part C of Medicare, is a plan offered by a private company that is approved by Medicare. Your monthly premium is your Part B premium and possibly an additional monthly premium, depending on your chosen plan.

When you enroll in a Medicare Advantage Plan, your Part B premium is sent to the company of your choice to pay for the cost. If you enroll in Medicare Advantage, you'll have:

- Part A Medicare/Hospital Insurance
- Part B Medicare/Doctors Insurance
- Part D Medicare/Prescription Drug Coverage (Most Plans)
- Some Extra Benefits Not Included in Parts A, B, or D

One of the main reasons people choose to get Medicare Advantage is because of the extra coverage and benefits associated with this private insurance plan. Some of the many coverage areas that are included in Part C but not other Medicare plans include vision, dental, over-the-counter products, gym memberships, and even hearing aids.

You may often be limited to the doctors included in your plan. Medicare Advantage can be an HMO or PPO plan.

Some people also have to get approval for specific medications or services before purchasing or receiving care. There are also different out-of-pocket costs that differ from Original Medicare. Many times, you pay a copay at the time of service.

PART D: PRESCRIPTION DRUG COVERAGE AND WHAT IT COSTS

The next part of Medicare you can add to your Parts A and B is Part D or prescription drug coverage. You can also receive this insurance by signing up for Medicare Advantage, which often includes this prescription coverage as part of their private insurance plans.

This is the insurance you'll need to cover the cost of prescription drugs. Part D assists in covering the cost of prescription drugs and is managed by private insurance companies approved by Medicare.

Regarding how much it costs, Part D sometimes has a monthly premium. Much like Medicare Advantage, you get to choose your plan, and that plan determines whether you have a premium or not. You can browse Medicare.gov to view all of the Part D and Part C plans available in your ZIP code and county.

Part D covers only prescription medications. Each plan has a formulary, which lists the drugs covered by that particular insurance company. You can choose the plan that works best for you and will cover what you need. Not every insurance company will cover every drug, so you'll need to shop around and choose an appropriate plan for you. Starting in 2025, the max out-of-pocket to the individual is $2,000 annually. The donut hole or coverage gap has been eliminated.

Each medication will be sorted into a tier, and each tier will have a copay or co-insurance (a percentage) associated with it that will vary from company to company. Here are the tiers:

- **Tier 1:** Preferred Generic
- **Tier 2:** Generic
- **Tier 3:** Preferred Name Brand
- **Tier 4:** Name Brand
- **Tier 5:** Specialty
- **Tier 6:** Insulin, which is capped at $35 due to the Inflation Reduction Act.

WHAT IS IRMAA: INCOME-RELATED MONTHLY ADJUSTMENT AMOUNT?

As mentioned when discussing Parts B and D, IRMAA or Income-Related Monthly Adjustment Amount is an additional charge you might have to pay based on your income. The good news is that this will only apply to Part B and D if you are above a certain threshold.

The amount is based on your tax return from two years ago. That means if you apply in 2025 for Medicare, you'll have an additional charge based on your 2023 tax returns. You can view the thresholds and their adjustments every year online, as they are published every year.

The threshold amounts are determined by the Social Security Office. Once you retire and your income decreases, you can visit your local Social Security Office to request an adjustment.

Remember, the base amount for everyone on Part B of Medicare is $185.00 per month. The IRMMA is added to the $185.00. These numbers change yearly, so it is best to keep up-to-date by reviewing the Medicare official data when it is released. Your IRMAA fee is also based on modified adjusted gross income, meaning that this is the amount you made after deductions on your tax returns. Capital gains are included as part of your income, as are the taxable portion of your Social Security benefits. The notice you receive is from the Social Security Office, and any discrepancies must be addressed with them.

Projected IRMAA for 2025

Single	Married filing jointly	Part B Income-Related Monthly Adjustment Amount	Part D Income-Related Monthly Adjustment Amount
Less than or equal to $105,000	Less than or equal to $210,000	$0.00	$0.00
Greater than $105,000 and less than or equal to $131,000	Greater than $210,000 and less than or equal to $262,000	$74.00	$13.70
Greater than $131,000 and less than or equal to $163,000	Greater than $262,000 and less than or equal to $326,000	$184.00	$35.30
Greater than $163,000 and less than or equal to $196,000	Greater than $326,000 and less than or equal to $392,000	$295.80	$57.00
Greater than $196,000 and less than or equal to $500,000	Greater than $392,000 and less than or equal to $750,000	$406.90	$78.60
Greater than or equal to $500,000	Greater than or equal to $750,000	$443.90	$85.80

Remember, the base amount for everyone on Part B of Medicare is $185.00 per month. The IRMMA is added to the $185.00.

Adapted from CMS.gov © Christine Ames LLC

Medicare premiums aren't one-size-fits-all—higher earners pay more, thanks to the Income-Related Monthly Adjustment Amount (IRMAA). Check the chart. If you make $105,000 or less as an individual ($210,000 or less for couples), you'll pay the standard $185 per month for Part B—no extra charges. But if your income goes up, so do your premiums. Earn between $131,000 and $163,000? You'll owe an extra $184 per month for Part B and $35.30 for Part D. The highest earners—over $500,000 single or $750,000 joint—will fork over $443.90 extra per month for Part B and $85.80 for Part D. These surcharges aren't optional—they're added directly to your Medicare premiums. If your income is close to these thresholds, planning ahead is key to avoid sticker shock when your Medicare bill arrives.

DO I HAVE TO TAKE MY SS BENEFIT TO ENROLL IN MEDICARE?

One of the most common questions seniors have regarding Medicare is if they must take their Social Security benefits to enroll in Medicare. The answer is no. They are separate, but you will receive a quarterly bill for your monthly premium until you withdraw your monthly Social Security check. If you draw your Social Security, then the government will automatically deduct the money from your check to pay for your Part B premium.

In other words, you do not have to start Social Security to receive Medicare A and B coverage. You can still get

Medicare and not be receiving Social Security. This allows for some flexibility that can help you decide when you want to start receiving your Social Security benefits based on your financial situation and retirement plan.

MEDICARE MIGHT BE COMPLEX, BUT IT IS HERE TO HELP YOU

While there are many moving parts to Medicare, this chapter hopefully provided a clear understanding of the basics. Medicare is not free, as there are some parts you have to pay for. Additionally, you might have to pay more than others if you are above a certain income threshold. You might even want to opt for Part C, or private health insurance, to receive more extra benefits.

As we continue to the next chapter, we'll explore your options as you reach 65. You're thinking about retiring and leaving your job, but is it the best option for you? We'll explore what to do if you're still working, what options you can choose from as you prepare for this next stage of your life, and how to make the best decision for your family.

CHAPTER 2

I Am Still Working and Turning 65

If you're reading this and still working, you might wonder if you have to enroll in Medicare. The truth is it depends. Not everyone benefits from enrolling in Medicare at the age of 65. However, for some, the cost of their group benefits is more expensive than the Medicare premiums. Your situation is likely not the same as a friend's, which is why you need to assess your needs before you make your decision.

This chapter will take a look at whether or not it is a good idea for you to enroll in Medicare or if it is better for you to wait until your situation has changed. To help you understand if enrolling in Medicare is the best option for you, we'll go through some questions to help you determine if you should keep your group benefits or if Medicare is a better option. So, use the actionable worksheet provided at the end of this chapter.

THE FIRST QUESTIONS FOR HUMAN RESOURCES

To get started, you need to assess your group benefits, your spouse's benefits, and their age, and whether you could get better coverage through Medicare. These are the main factors that will determine the best course of action for you and your spouse. Specifically, ask HR and yourself the following:

1. Can I stay in group medical even if I turn 65 and leave everything unchanged?
2. Are you required to enroll in Medicare A and B?
3. Does your premium change?
4. Do you have a spouse on the group benefit and under 65?

If you answer yes to question #4, staying with your group benefits is a good idea. You'll get better coverage in the long term for your spouse. Please read "What To Do If You Retire and Your Spouse Is Under 65" for more information about your options.

If you are able to continue on the group, that is generally the best choice for spouses under the age of 65. If this sounds like your situation, it's best to wait until you are both 65 years of age or older to consider switching from your group benefit to Medicare.

The next area of concern is if opting out of your group benefits is a permanent decision. We'll also look at issues like cost, including your deductible, what medications you're taking, and more to determine if Medicare would cover just as much for a lower cost than your group benefits. Let's go over some more questions to ask HR Resources before you formally make your healthcare choice for you or your family.

THE SECOND SET OF QUESTIONS TO ASK HUMAN RESOURCES

Now, another area of concern is whether or not dropping your group benefits now means losing them permanently. You also need to understand if your monthly premium and overall healthcare costs would reduce if you switched to Medicare from your group benefits. Before we get any further, answer this question on your worksheet:

- If I leave the group, can I get back in next year? Is this a permanent decision?

Choosing to leave your group benefits might mean that you lose the group insurance benefits permanently. There are some plans that will not allow you to re-enroll.

The question to answer is whether this is cost-effective for you. The most important thing to consider is not only how much it costs you. To determine if keeping your group benefits is better, here are some questions you'll need to answer accurately. Please fill in these questions on the worksheet provided at the end of the chapter:

- What is the monthly premium for the group plan?
- What is the annual deductible?
- What is the Max Out of Pocket?
- What is the maximum payout for your Plan?
- What is your copay for PCP, Specialist, MRI, Chemotherapy, Radiation Treatment, and Overnight in a Hospital?
- What medications are you currently taking, and how many are name-brand?
- What is the total monthly cost of your medications?

You might not think these are important to answer, but they are key determinants in whether or not switching to Medicare is better for you. For example, let's say that your monthly premium is lower for the group plan than it would be for Medicare, but you might have a hefty deductible that is expensive.

To look at your potential costs, calculate how much you spend monthly on medications. Look at your total monthly expense, what your annual deductible is, and your max out-of-pocket. You also need to look at your copay. Compare the numbers to that of the potential Medicare plans you might choose.

You'll be able to easily determine if group benefits are better than Medicare or vice versa. It's all about seeing what is the most cost-effective. By using the worksheet provided, you'll be able to make a side-by-side comparison to see it all plainly so you can make your choice.

WHAT TO DO IF YOU RETIRE AND YOUR SPOUSE IS UNDER 65

If you have retired or plan to retire and your spouse is under 65, the best choice is to enroll your spouse in an ACA plan while you enroll in Medicare. ACA, or the Affordable Care Act, was introduced as Obama Care in 2010 and is found at Healthcare.gov. ACA plans are great for covering all of the pre-existing conditions, and there are no medical questions required. Your premium is determined based on your gender, age, and smoker status. This makes it incredibly easy to sign up, so it can often be a viable option for some.

However, finding affordable plans has not always been easy. It is easy to apply but can be expensive for some. Depending on your income level, you may get a subsidy from the government. Yet, it's important to explore all of your local options to ensure you find the best coverage. An ACA Insurance Agent can guide you if you are not computer savvy or call Healthcare.gov directly.

As for you, since you are retired and of age, you can enroll in Medicare A and B. Then, you can choose a Medicare Supplement plan or Medicare Advantage if you prefer that instead. Now, let's talk about what to do if your spouse is turning 65 and you're the one still working.

WHAT TO DO IF YOUR SPOUSE IS TURNING 65, YOU'RE STILL WORKING AND YOU ARE UNDER 65

If your spouse is turning 65 and you're still working, then it's time to look at the cost of the group benefits for your spouse. In general, you can expect the employer to pay a good portion or all of the employees' costs for their healthcare premiums. However, that is not always the case for the spouse. You generally pay more for the spouse to be on the group benefit. It is essential to ask HR what amount you pay monthly for your spouse.

In this situation, use the worksheet to figure out all of your overall costs. You'll need to review some of the answers to the questions we explored in the second part and your completed worksheet. Then, you'll be able to see what is the most cost-effective, as well as what is the best plan for your situation in the event you retire soon.

WHAT TO DO: IF YOU CONTINUE WORKING, STAY ON THE GROUP PLAN FOR YOU AND YOUR SPOUSE

If you plan to continue working even after you've reached

65, then you should enroll in Medicare A only and keep your group benefits. You might be wondering why since Medicare typically replaces your group benefit. However, in some cases, you might get better coverage and be able to enjoy more benefits without paying more each month for a new premium.

As we discussed in Chapter 1, there is a monthly premium for Part B of Medicare, not Part A. By only enrolling in Part A, you are ensuring you defer your Part B enrollment till you are ready to retire and not paying unnecessary monthly premiums. That means you can enjoy Medicare Part A for zero premium and keep your group benefits. Your group would continue to be primary, and Part A of Medicare would be secondary. If you do choose to keep your group plan, be sure to read more on "creditable coverage" in Chapter 3. This is extremely important.

By following this path, you're essentially delaying your enrollment in Part B of Medicare and boosting your overall coverage in the process without paying a cent more than you already are.

WHAT TO DO IF YOU'RE RETIRED AND HAVE LIFETIME BENEFITS AVAILABLE FROM YOUR GROUP BENEFITS

If you're retired, you might have group benefits from your employer that you can access. This is a question for HR, as they will be able to access this information so you can make a decision and understand what's available to you. In this situation, you'll also have to ask if you enroll in Medicare Part B and pay the premium, which insurance will be the primary?

In most cases, your Medicare—even if you have group benefits—will be the primary. This makes your group benefits secondary. You also should ask HR if this means that your group premium then gets reduced. With Medicare being primary, it significantly reduces the cost to the employer. You should definitely see some type of reduction in your premium. The best way to figure this out is to use the worksheet that we have available to do the math.

There are both excellent group plans and bad group plans. It all depends on the size of the group. With help from HR and your own worksheet calculations, you can see what you'll likely pay if you have any outstanding group benefits and what would be best for you and your spouse. Your decision will be different from others, so take the time to look at all the details before you and your spouse decide what to do.

WHAT TO DO IF YOU'RE BOTH 65 OR OLDER

If you and your spouse are both over the age of 65, then it's time to consider taking both you and your spouse over to Medicare and off of Group. When your spouse turns 65, it's time to look at open enrollment. We'll talk more about this in Chapter 9 and what you'll need to do. However, before you jump in, you'll need to assess your situation.

As with the other options, take the time to go through the worksheet. You have all of the numbers there, and you can determine what Medicare plans would be best for you. Generally, you and your spouse will typically get better coverage for less money when you're both over the age of 65.

One question people often have at this stage is whether it is better to retire or continue working. You can still work and enjoy Medicare benefits. Consider keeping your dental and vision insurance through your employer. They are typically separate from your group medical plan and are inexpensive, offering good coverage.

WHAT TO DO IF YOUR EMPLOYER REQUIRES YOU TO ENROLL IN MEDICARE A & B

Some employers require employees to enroll in Medicare Parts A and B in order to remain on the group health plan. This practice is becoming more common because it shifts the cost burden, making Medicare the primary payer and reducing employer expenses. However, while this may save money for your employer, it may not be the best choice for you.

If you're turning 65 and enrolling in Medicare Part B, this is your open enrollment period (see Chapter 9). This means you have the right to enroll in any Medicare plan with no medical underwriting—a unique opportunity that you lose if you enroll in Medicare Part B through your employer and keep your group benefits.

While employers often reduce your group premium when you enroll in Medicare, you will still have to pay your Part B premium, and your benefits may not be as strong as those of a traditional Medicare Supplement plan (see Chapter 6).

If you have a chronic condition such as diabetes, heart disease, or COPD, protecting your open enrollment rights is even more important. If you want to stay with group, delay Medicare B enrollment and keep your group health plan as your primary coverage.

Before making a final decision, check with HR to confirm:

- Whether you must enroll in Medicare Part B
- How your group premium will change if you enroll
- If your group benefits provide comparable coverage to Medicare

By asking the right questions and carefully weighing your options, you can make the best decision for your health and finances.

It all depends on what you have discovered by completing the worksheet and going through the questions and issues we explored.

TURNING 65
You turn 65 in May

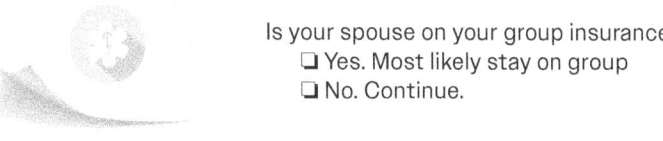

Is your spouse on your group insurance and under 65?
❏ Yes. Most likely stay on group
❏ No. Continue.

What is the monthly premium for your group insurance? _____
Pleae note not per pay check but monthly

What is the Medical Annual deductible? _____

What is the Medical Max out-of-pocket? _____

Copay for Specialist? _____

Copay for overnight in the Hospital? _____

Diagnostic Test, X-ray or Blood Work _____

Imaging: CT Scan, PET Scan, MRI _____

Deductible for Medications _____

Monthly Cost for Medications _____

Monthly Cost for Group Insurance _____

Estimate Annual Cost:

   Monthly Premium x 12 _____

   Monthly Medications x 12 _____

   Deductible _____

   Total Annual Cost _____

Worst Case Senario
Add Max Out of Pocket _____
To Annual Cost Above

© Copyright 2025 by Christine Ames and Christine Ames, LLC

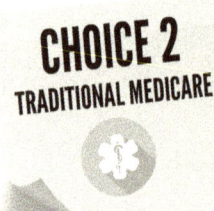

CHOICE 2 — TRADITIONAL MEDICARE

- TRADITIONAL MEDICARE - ENROLL IN MEDICARE A & B
- ENROLL IN A MEDICARE SUPPLEMENT PLAN G - See Chapter Six for Details
- ENROLL IN A STAND ALONE PRESCRIPTION DRUG CARD
- INDIVIDUAL WITH NO IRMMA

PART A OF MEDICARE	$0.00	
PART B OF MEDICARE, Monthly	$185.00	
Medicare Supplement Plan G	*1	Monthly cost for Plan G in your zip code
PART D OF MEDICARE Prescription Drug Program	*2	Monthly cost for Prescription Drug Plan in your zip code
What is the Medical Annual deductible?	$257.00	Fixed for 2025
What is the Medical Max out-of-pocket?	$0.00	Fixed for 2025
Copay for Specialist?	$0.00	Fixed for 2025
Copay for overnight in the Hospital?	$0.00	Fixed for 2025
Diagnostic Test, X-ray or Blood Work	$0.00	Fixed for 2025
Imaging: CT Scan, PET Scan, MRI	$0.00	Fixed for 2025
Chemo or Radiation	$0.00	Fixed for 2025
Deductible for Medications Deductible only applies towards meds in Tier 3, 4 and 5	$590.00	Fixed for 2025 (this is included in max 2k)
Medications: Max Pay Out for Meds.	$2,000.00	Fixed for 2025 (this includes your premium)

Tier 1	Preferred Generic Copay	$0.00	Average Copay in USA
Tier 2	Generic Copay	$10.00	
Tier 3	Preferred Name Brand Copay	$45.00	
Tier 4	Name Brand Copay	$100.00	or percentage
Tier 5	Specialty Copay	25% Co Insurance	

© Copyright 2025 by Christine Ames and Christine Ames, LLC

Worst Case Scenario: Managing Chronic Illness with expensive medications or in the middle of chemo or radiation.

ANNUAL MAX OUT OF POCKET FOR THE YEAR:

PART A:	$0.00	Fixed for 2025
PART B:	$2,457.00	Fixed for 2025
PART D:	$2,000.00	Max Fixed Amount

Medicare Supplement _____ **YOUR ACTUAL COST**
*1. Monthly Amount x 12

_____ **YOUR ACTUAL COST**
Add: Part A, B, D & Medicare Supplement

Healthy: You only need maintenance medications, such as blood pressure and cholesterol, and annual check-ups.

ANNUAL MAX OUT OF POCKET FOR THE YEAR:

PART A:	$0.00	Fixed for 2025
PART B:	$2,457.00	Fixed for 2025
PART D:		**YOUR ACTUAL COST**

_____ *2. Monthly Amount x 12

Medicare Supplement _____ **YOUR ACTUAL COST**
*1. Monthly Amount x 12

_____ **YOUR ACTUAL COST**
Add: Part A, B, D & Medicare Supplement

Compare:

Group Estimated Annual Cost
(see calculation from Choice 1) _____

Traditional Medicare Annual Cost
Medicare Supplement Plan G
Worst Case _____

Traditional Medicare Annual Cost
Medicare Supplement Plan G
Healthy _____

> Compare

© Copyright 2025 by Christine Ames and Christine Ames, LLC

CHOICE 3
MEDICARE ADVANTAGE

ENROLL IN
- MEDICARE ADVANTAGE PLAN - See Chapter 7 for Details
- INDIVIDUAL WITH NO IRMMA

* Medicare.gov will give you this information or a local agent

PART A OF MEDICARE	$0.00	
PART B OF MEDICARE, Monthly	$185.00	
Monthly Premium for Medicare Advantage	_____	**Monthly premium for plan in your zip code**
PART D OF MEDICARE included in Medicare Advantage		
What is the Medical Annual deductible?	_____	
What is the Medical Max out-of-pocket?	_____ *2	
Copay for Specialist?	_____	**Fill in dollar amounts for plan in your zip code from Medicare.gov**
Copay for overnight in the Hospital?	_____	
Diagnostic Test, X-ray or Blood Work	_____	
Imaging: CT Scan, PET Scan, MRI	_____	
Chemo or Radiation	20% CoInsurance	You would hit your Medical Max out-of-pocket
Deductible for Medications Deductible only applies towards meds in Tier 3,4 and 5	_____	**Fill in dollar amount**
Medications: Max Pay Out for Meds.	$2,000.00	Fixed for 2025 (this includes your premium)

Tier 1	Preferred Generic Copay	$0.00	**Medicare.gov will give you an estimated dollar amount**
Tier 2	Generic Copay	$10.00	
Tier 3	Preferred Name Brand Copay	$45.00	
Tier 4	Name Brand Copay	$100.00	
Tier 5	Specialty Copay	25% Co Insurance	

_____ *1   **Monthly cost of your medications**

© Copyright 2025 by Christine Ames and Christine Ames, LLC

Worst Case Scenario: Managing Chronic Illness with expensive Tier 4 medications or in the middle of chemo or radiation.

ANNUAL MAX OUT OF POCKET FOR THE YEAR:

PART A:	$0.00	Fixed for 2025
PART B:	$2,200.00	Fixed for 2025
PART D:	$2,000.00	Max Fixed Amount

Max Out of Pocket for your Plan
_____ *2. Dollar Amount

YOUR ACTUAL COST
_____ Add: Part A, B, D & Max Out of Pocket

Healthy: You only need maintenance medications, such as blood pressure and cholesterol, and annual check-ups.

ANNUAL MAX OUT OF POCKET FOR THE YEAR:

PART A:	$0.00	Fixed for 2025
PART B:	$2,200.00	Fixed for 2025
PART D:		**YOUR ACTUAL COST**

_____ *1. Monthly Amount x 12

YOUR ACTUAL COST
_____ Add: Part A, B, D

Compare:

Group Estimated Annual Cost
(see calculation from Choice 1)   _____

*Medicare Advantage
Annual Cost*
Worst Case   _____   Compare

*Medicare Advantage
Annual Cost*
Healthy   _____

© Copyright 2025 by Christine Ames and Christine Ames, LLC

CHAPTER 3

How Can I Avoid Medicare Penalties and Creditable Coverage

Turning 65 comes with big decisions—one of the most important is whether to enroll in Medicare. Making the right choice ensures you get the healthcare coverage you need while avoiding costly penalties. But do you need to enroll right away? What happens if you wait?

This chapter breaks down everything you need to know, including what creditable coverage is, how it affects your enrollment, and the consequences of delaying Medicare Parts B and D. By the end, you'll have a clear understanding of the steps to take, the deadlines to watch, and how to make the smartest choice for your healthcare future.

UNDERSTANDING CREDIBLE COVERAGE

When it comes to Medicare, timing matters. One of the most important factors in avoiding unnecessary penalties is creditable coverage—but what exactly does that mean? If you're delaying Part B and Part D of Medicare, you need to know whether your current or past health insurance meets Medicare's standards.

What is Creditable Coverage?

Creditable coverage refers to any health plan that provides benefits equal to or better than Medicare's standard prescription drug coverage (Part D). If you have or had insurance that meets these criteria, you won't be penalized for delaying Medicare enrollment.

Common types of creditable coverage include:

- **Employer Group Insurance** – Many retirees stay on their employer's or spouse's workplace health plan.
- **Veterans Affairs (VA) Benefits** – VA healthcare plans typically offer prescription drug coverage that meets Medicare's requirements.
- **TRICARE** – A government healthcare program for active-duty and retired service members and their families.

If you're covered under one of these plans, you can delay

Medicare Part B and Part D without penalty. However, not all employer or retiree plans qualify—so it's important to confirm with your provider.

Why Is It Important?

Having creditable coverage is essential if you want to adhere to Medicare's rules but also to protect your wallet. Here's why it's so important:

- **Avoid Late Enrollment Penalties** – If you don't sign up for Medicare Part D when first eligible and don't have creditable coverage, you'll be charged an extra 1% on your Part D premium for every month you delay. This penalty never goes away, meaning you'll pay more for as long as you have Medicare.
- **Required Proof for Medicare** – Medicare doesn't automatically know if you had creditable coverage. You'll need a creditable coverage letter from your employer or benefits provider to prove you were covered and avoid penalties.

How to Obtain a Creditable Coverage Letter

If you delayed enrollment in Medicare, you'll need a creditable coverage letter to prove your prior coverage. You won't need this if you're turning 65 years old and enroll right away. However, if you need it, here's how to get one:

Requesting the Letter from HR or Your Employer

1. **Contact Your HR Department** – Request the letter well before you transition to Medicare to avoid delays.
2. **Specify Your Needs** – Ask for a letter that confirms your coverage met Medicare's requirements.

A **valid** creditable coverage letter should include:

- **Start and end dates** of your group coverage.
- **Employer's letterhead** and official **signature** (Medicare does not accept unsigned or unofficial letters).

Why You Need a Hard Copy

Medicare does not accept electronic copies, emails, or faxes for proof of coverage. You'll need a hard copy to submit to the Social Security Administration. You should also keep an extra copy for your records in case it's ever needed again.

What to Do if Your Employer is Going Out of Business

If your employer is closing or has already shut down, act fast to secure your creditable coverage letter.

- **Request It ASAP** – If your company is still operating, contact HR immediately to get the letter before they close.

- **If HR Is Unavailable** – Reach out to a former supervisor or company executive who may still have access to records.

Without this letter, proving your coverage later could be difficult, leaving you stuck with permanent Medicare penalties.

MEDICARE PART D LATE ENROLLMENT PENALTY

When it comes to Medicare, timing is everything—especially when enrolling in Part D, which covers prescription drugs. If you miss your initial enrollment window, you could face a lifelong penalty that increases your monthly premium. Fortunately, this penalty is avoidable if you take the right steps.

In this section, we'll break down what the Part D penalty is, how it's calculated, and most importantly, how to avoid it. If you've already been hit with the penalty, we'll also cover your options for reducing medication costs.

What is the Part D Penalty?

Medicare Part D is designed to help you cover the cost of prescription drugs. But here's the catch: If you don't enroll when you're first eligible and don't have creditable drug coverage, you'll pay more—every month, for life.

So, how is the penalty calculated?

- For every month you go without Part D or creditable drug coverage, Medicare adds a 1% penalty per month to your premium.
- The penalty is actually based on the national base beneficiary premium, which changes yearly.
- The longer you wait, the higher your penalty.

For example, if you delay enrollment for five years (60 months), your penalty will be 60% of the national base premium.

- If the base premium is $33.06, your extra monthly cost would be $19.84 ($33.06 × 0.60).
- This penalty is added to your regular premium and never goes away unless you qualify for financial assistance.

How to Avoid the Part D Penalty

The good news is that you can avoid this penalty entirely with proper planning. Here's how:

1. **Enroll in a Part D Plan at 65**
   - Your Initial Enrollment Period (IEP) begins three months before you turn 65 and then ends three months after your birth month. Enroll during this window to avoid penalties.
2. **Make Sure Your Employer Coverage Qualifies**
   - If you're still working and have employer-provided

insurance, check if your plan includes creditable prescription drug coverage (meaning it's at least as good as Medicare's Part D).
- Ask HR for a creditable coverage letter to keep on file in case Medicare asks for proof later.

3. **Consider Veterans Affairs (VA) or Other Coverage**
    - If you have VA benefits, your drug coverage is creditable, meaning you won't need Part D unless you want additional coverage.
    - Employer retiree plans may also count as creditable coverage, but you should verify this before delaying enrollment.

What to Do If You Already Have a Part D Penalty

If you've already missed your enrollment period and don't have creditable coverage, you may be stuck with the penalty—but that doesn't mean you don't have options.

1. Medicare Advantage Plans Without Part D

Some Medicare Advantage (Part C) plans do not include Part D coverage. These plans are often marketed toward veterans or individuals who get their prescriptions covered elsewhere.

- **Pros:** No Part D penalty.
- **Cons:** You'll have to find another way to pay for prescriptions, such as through discount programs.

2. Prescription Discount Programs

Many people with a Part D penalty lower their out-of-pocket costs using GoodRx, Costco, or other pharmacy discount cards.

- These programs aren't insurance, but they often provide savings on medications.
- Some retirees also purchase medications from Canada or other international pharmacies where drug prices may be lower.

3. Weigh the Pros and Cons of Medicare Advantage Without Part D

While skipping Part D may seem appealing to avoid the penalty, there are downsides:

- You may end up paying more for medications out-of-pocket than if you enrolled in Part D.
- Certain medications may be much cheaper with Medicare's negotiated rates.

PART D CREDITABLE COVERAGE VERIFICATION LETTER

Once you enroll in Medicare Part D, your plan provider—such as Humana or UnitedHealthcare (UHC)—will send you a verification letter. This letter confirms whether you had creditable prescription drug coverage before enrolling in Part D.

Why does this matter? If Medicare doesn't receive proof that you had creditable coverage, you could be stuck with a late enrollment penalty—even if you shouldn't owe one. That's why responding to this letter on time is critical.

What To Do When You Receive the Letter

When your verification letter arrives, don't set it aside—act immediately. Here's what you need to do:

1. Fill out the form completely. Provide details about your previous prescription drug coverage, including:
    - Your insurance provider
    - Your policy number
    - The dates your coverage was active
2. Attach any requested documentation. If Medicare asks for proof, submit a copy of your creditable coverage letter from your employer or insurance provider.
3. Follow the return instructions. You may need to mail or call customer service—pay attention to the details.
4. If mailing, consider using tracking. This ensures your response is received and processed.

Avoid These Common Mistakes

- **Ignoring the letter**. Failing to respond will automatically trigger a penalty—even if you had creditable coverage.

- **Submitting incomplete information.** Missing details could delay verification, leading to unnecessary charges.
- **Missing the deadline.** Medicare enforces strict timeframes—don't wait until the last minute.

By handling this process promptly and correctly, you can protect yourself from costly penalties and keep your Medicare Part D coverage running smoothly.

MEDICARE PART B LATE ENROLLMENT PENALTY

Medicare Part B covers essential medical services like doctor visits, outpatient care, and preventive screenings. But if you delay enrollment without creditable coverage, you could face a permanent late enrollment penalty—increasing your monthly premium for life.

This section explains who is affected, how the penalty is calculated, and—most importantly—how to avoid it.

What is the Part B Penalty?

If you don't choose to sign up for Medicare Part B when you're first eligible at age 65 and don't have creditable coverage, Medicare adds a 10% penalty to your monthly premium for every full year you delay enrollment. Here's an example:

- If you delay Part B enrollment for three years, you'll pay 30% more—permanently.
- With a standard Part B premium of $185 per month, your new monthly cost would be $240.50 ($185 + 30%).

Unlike the Part D penalty**,** which affects prescription drug coverage, this penalty applies to your medical benefits and lasts as long as you have Medicare.

Who Is Affected by the Part B Penalty?

You won't face a Part B penalty if:

- You're covered under an employer-sponsored health plan (yours or your spouse's).

However, if you retire, lose job-based insurance, or go uninsured after age 65 without enrolling in Part B, you'll be penalized**.** That's why it's critical to get a verification letter from your employer confirming your coverage.

How to Avoid the Part B Penalty

- **Enroll in Part B at 65** unless you have creditable employer coverage.
- **If you have employer coverage**, request a written verification letter from HR to confirm it's creditable.

- **When your employee coverage ends, you'll need to sign up for Part B immediately** and start the Part B enrollment process before your retirement date.

By planning ahead, you can ensure you protect yourself from lifelong higher premiums and ensure seamless healthcare coverage.

SPECIAL SITUATIONS AND RECOMMENDATIONS

When it comes to Medicare enrollment, not all situations are the same. Some employers require Medicare enrollment, while others offer lifetime benefits. If you're married, you may need to coordinate coverage with your spouse. Let's break down what to consider in each case.

When Your Employer Requires Medicare Enrollment

Some employers mandate that employees enroll in Medicare Parts A and B once they turn 65—often to reduce company healthcare costs. If this applies to you, talk to your HR department to understand how this impacts your coverage. Here are some questions you'll want to ask them:

- How will Medicare A & B affect my group insurance premiums?

- Will my group plan still offer comparable benefits?
- Can I drop my group plan later without penalties?

Knowing these answers will help you make the best financial decision for your healthcare needs.

What to Do If You Are Retiring and Have Lifetime Group Benefits

Some retirees continue receiving health benefits from their former employer. If this applies to you, find out:

- Will Medicare or my group plan be my primary coverage?
- Will my premiums decrease once Medicare takes over as the primary payer?

Use a cost-comparison worksheet to see if keeping your group benefits or switching fully to Medicare makes more sense.

CONCLUSION AND FINAL STEPS

Now that you understand creditable coverage and how to avoid costly penalties, you're in a strong position to make informed Medicare decisions. The next step is enrollment—and knowing when and how to sign up is just as important.

In Chapter 4, we'll break down the practical steps to enrolling in Medicare, whether you're opting for Part A only or both Parts A and B. You'll also explore the three main enrollment options to ensure you decide on the best option for your healthcare needs.

CHAPTER 4

How to Enroll in Medicare

Turning 65 brings a lot of big decisions—one of the most important is enrolling in Medicare. The process itself isn't necessarily difficult, but timing and method matter. Should you enroll online, over the phone, or in person? What happens if you only need Part A for now? And what should you expect if you delayed Part B and need to enroll later?

The truth is that enrolling in Medicare can be straightforward or a frustrating waiting game, depending on your situation. Because this process involves government agencies, you'll want to be proactive, organized, and patient.

In this chapter, we'll walk you through your enrollment options step by step. By the end, you'll know exactly which method is best for your situation and how to avoid common pitfalls.

THE THREE WAYS TO ENROLL IN MEDICARE

First, you have three main ways to enroll in Medicare:

- **Online** – The easiest and fastest method (if it applies to you).
- **Phone** – A good option for those who prefer talking to a representative or need additional paperwork.
- **In-Person** – Ideal for those with complex enrollment situations or who prefer face-to-face assistance.

Each option has both pros and cons, depending on your circumstances. Let's break them down and explore which option would be best for you based on your situation.

CHOICE 1: ENROLLING ONLINE (THE FASTEST OPTION)

If you want to enroll in Medicare as quickly and easily as possible, applying online is your best bet. The Social Security Administration (SSA) allows you to apply through its website, www.ssa.gov.

This method is best for a specific group of people. If you are:

- Turning 65 and enrolling in both Medicare Parts A and B
- Enrolling in only Part A (because you have creditable coverage)
- Wanting to avoid the wait times at your local Social Security offices

Who Can't Use This Method?

Unfortunately, not everyone can just enroll online. For those who are delaying enrollment into Part B and need to sign up now, you cannot use the online process. Instead, you'll have to apply by phone or in person, which will be explored later.

How to Apply Online: A Step-By-Step Guide

First, go to www.ssa.gov. Next, you'll want to click on the "Medicare" tab at the top of the page. After that, you'll need to log into My Social Security account. Those who do not have one of these accounts can create one before you proceed. It is an easy process and should not take too long to set up.

Once you have your My Social Security account set up, you'll need to select "Apply for Medicare." Then, follow the on-screen instructions and fill out the required details. Once you have filled out all of the required fields and double-checked that your information is correct, hit "Submit Your Application."

After submitting your application, you'll receive a confirmation email from the Social Security Administration.

What Happens Next?

Once your application is submitted, it should take only 3-4 weeks for you to receive your Medicare card and number in the mail. You can always log onto your My Social Security account if you want to check the status of your Medicare application before then.

If you need to get a Medicare number ASAP for any reason, call 1-800-MEDICARE after you get approved to get your claim number before your card arrives. That way, you can enroll in a plan that goes with Medicare without waiting.

CHOICE 2: ENROLLING BY PHONE

If you're not comfortable enrolling online or if your enrollment requires additional paperwork, applying by phone is another option. This is best for those who:

- Don't use computers or prefer speaking to a representative
- Have delayed enrollment into Part B because of employer coverage
- Need extra forms mailed to them to fill out

How to Apply by Phone: A Step-By-Step Guide

To apply by phone, all you have to do is call your local Social Security Office. Simply tell them that you want to enroll in Medicare Part A and B, or just Part A if that applies to your situation.

They'll have you schedule an appointment. The Social Security representative will take your application over the phone verbally. This is a recorded call. Your appointment may be scheduled 2-4 weeks later, depending on the season. Some times of the year, it is harder to get an appointment, while others may have earlier appointments available.

If you're calling from October to December, it is the busiest time, so don't delay your application! Try to schedule your appointment during other times throughout the year so you can avoid long wait times.

For Those Who Delayed Part B Enrollment

If you have delayed Part B enrollment due to having a current employer plan, you will need to provide additional paperwork for your Medicare enrollment. Before you come to your appointment, please prepare the following:

- A proof of coverage letter from your employer (See Chapter 3 for details)
- A completed CMS-40B (Application for Enrollment in Medicare Part B) form
- A completed CMS-L564 (Request for Employment Information) form

Both of these forms are available online in PDF format. You can fill them out ahead of time. However, they must be returned by mail or given in person, as Social Security does not accept emails or faxes. Make sure you do this ahead of time to avoid any unnecessary delays.

Ensure you have copies of everything you send, too. If your documents get lost, it can delay your enrollment for months, leading to issues and barriers to Medicare coverage.

CHOICE 3: ENROLLING IN-PERSON

For those who would rather meet face-to-face for assistance, visiting a local Social Security office is another option. You don't have to rely on calling or applying online. There should be a local office near you that can help you complete your Medicare enrollment.

Who Should Use This Method?

If you want to speak with someone in person, need help with extra forms, or are enrolling Part B after delaying and needing to submit paperwork, this is your best option for Medicare enrollment.

How to Apply In-Person: A Step-By-Step Guide

First, you'll need to find your nearest SSA Office. You can use the office locator at www.ssa.gov to find the nearest office to your home. Then, it's highly recommended to make an appointment beforehand.

You don't have to make an appointment, as they do accept walk-ins. However, walk-ins might be subject to waiting several hours. When you make an appointment ahead of time, you can save hours and cut down your wait time significantly.

Ahead of your appointment, don't forget to prepare the right files and bring them. If you are enrolling in Part B, you need to bring the following documents:

- Proof of creditable coverage letter
- CMS-40B and CMS L564 forms

If you are just enrolling in Part A, you'll need to only bring your Social Security number.

For those who live in rural areas, you're in luck! Rural Social Security offices are generally less crowded than city offices. If you live near a smaller town, you might want to consider driving there to avoid the wait.

HOW TO GET HELP WITH YOUR APPLICATION

- **Phone:** Call Social Security at 1-800-772-1213. TTY users should call 1-800-325-0778.
- **En español:** Llame a SSA gratis al 1-800-772-1213 y oprima el 2 si desea el servicio en español y espere a que le atienda un agente.
- **In-person:** Your local Social Security office. For an office near you, check ssa.gov/locator.

HOW TO GET YOUR MEDICARE CLAIM NUMBER

After you apply, you'll receive a Medicare Claim Number (a mix of numbers and letters). You'll need this number because:

- You can't enroll in a Medicare Supplement, Advantage Plan, or Part D plan without it
- Your healthcare providers will need it to bill Medicare

There are only three ways to get your Medicare Claim Number:

- **Log into My Social Security Account (Fastest):** Using this method, you can see your claim number clearly on your account and access it for what you need.
- **Call 1-800-MEDICARE:** If you don't want to use the computer, you can call, and they can provide your claim number over the phone. Just have a pen and paper ready.
- **Wait for Your Medicare Card:** Of course, you can always wait for your card. They will send it to you in a few weeks, and your number will be clearly listed on the card.

What To Do If You're Stuck Waiting for Your Medicare Card

Sometimes, Medicare can take a long time to send your card. Processing times are unpredictable, so if you haven't received your card and need your claim number urgently, there are a few things you can do.

First, you can call 1-800-MEDICARE. They will provide you with your claim number and start dates. All you'll have to do is write it down and keep it somewhere safe until your actual Medicare Claim Number and card come in the mail.

Otherwise, you can also check on www.ssa.gov. Your My Social Security account may display your claim number before your card arrives. Just be sure to keep it somewhere safe until you get your Medicare card.

It's important to have your Medicare Claim Number available, as you cannot enroll in a Medicare Supplement, Advantage Plan, or Part D Plan without this number. If you have to enroll in any of these plans, you first need to have your claim number and correct start dates for Parts A and B.

FINAL THOUGHTS: PICK THE BEST ENROLLMENT STRATEGY FOR YOU

You will have to decide what the best enrollment strategy is for you. Everyone's situation is different. However, to recap, if you're:

- **Turning 65 and Enrolling in Parts A and B:** Apply online for the fastest processing and to avoid long wait times at the local office.
- **Enrolling Now and Have Delayed Part B:** Apply by phone or in person, and be sure to prepare your documents ahead of time to avoid issues.
- **Dealing with a Complex Situation or Prefer In-Person Help:** Schedule an in-person appointment and be prepared for a small wait, or opt for a rural office.

With an understanding of these options and how to apply for Medicare, you can take care of the necessary paperwork and ensure you're all set, in compliance, and ready to use your claim number.

In Chapter 5, we'll explore the Inflation Reduction Act, its historical background, and its current impact. We'll also break down the 2025 changes, including the M3P Program, so you can stay informed about how these updates may affect your Medicare coverage and healthcare costs.

CHAPTER 5

Inflation Reduction Act

Medicare is changing—in a big way. If you're on Medicare, you've probably heard about the Inflation Reduction Act (IRA). Signed into law in 2022, this bill promises to lower prescription drug costs and reduce out-of-pocket expenses for millions of seniors. But what does it really mean for you?

The IRA brings some of the biggest changes to Medicare in nearly 20 years, with many key provisions kicking in by this year. Some of the most important updates include:

- A $2,000 annual cap on out-of-pocket drug costs (down from $8,000)
- The end of the Medicare Part D 'Donut Hole,' simplifying drug coverage
- A $35 cap on insulin for Medicare recipients
- Free vaccines for seniors, including the shingles vaccine

Fortunately, these updates will save millions of people money, but they also come with trade-offs. Since insurance companies are now covering more of the cost, some Medicare Advantage Plans may see higher premiums, added medication deductibles, hospital deductibles, or reduced benefits.

In this chapter, we'll break everything down step by step so you know exactly what's changing, how it affects you, and what to watch out for in 2026 and beyond. Let's start with discussing the price cap on insulin.

MAJOR MEDICARE CHANGES UNDER THE IRA: WHAT YOU NEED TO KNOW

#1: Insulin Price Cap

If you have diabetes, you know just how expensive insulin can be. For years, seniors on Medicare faced sky-high prices, often paying hundreds of dollars or more a month just to get the medication they needed to survive. Some people decided to ration their doses, skip injections, or simply struggled to afford other necessities just to pay for insulin.

That changed in 2023 when the Inflation Reduction Act introduced a $35 monthly cap on insulin for Medicare beneficiaries. This is a huge relief for the millions of seniors who rely on insulin to manage their blood sugar. Instead of unpredictable and overwhelming costs, Medicare recipients now have a fixed, manageable monthly expense.

So, what does this mean for you? Here's what you need to know:

- If you're on Medicare Part D or a Medicare Advantage plan with drug coverage, your insulin costs are capped at $35 per box of pens or vial of insulin—no surprises, no unexpected price jumps.
- If you take multiple types of insulin, each prescription is capped at $35, meaning more savings for those on multiple medications.
- If you're on private insurance (or have no coverage), this cap does NOT apply—but there are growing efforts to lower insulin prices across the board.

This change saves money, but more importantly, it's also saving lives. Many seniors who couldn't afford their full dose of insulin faced dangerous complications, including hospitalizations, nerve damage, and worsening diabetes. With this price cap in place, more Medicare recipients can now take their insulin as prescribed and avoid serious health risks.

What's Next?
The $35 cap is a major step, but it's only the beginning. Lawmakers are pushing for lower insulin prices for everyone, not just Medicare beneficiaries. For now, if you're on Medicare, this cap ensures that your insulin is affordable and predictable—no matter what!

#2: Free Vaccinations
Staying healthy is about treating illnesses but also taking

proactive steps to prevent them before they start. Thanks to the Inflation Reduction Act (IRA), those with Medicare no longer have to pay out-of-pocket for most recommended vaccines. As of 2023, important immunizations you need, like shingles, flu, tetanus, and pneumonia, are now completely free under Medicare.

For many seniors, including you, this is an amazing change. Before this, vaccines like the shingles shot could cost over $200, making it too expensive for many people to get. That meant some seniors had to take the risk of skipping essential vaccines simply because of the cost.

Now, you don't have to worry about that. If you're on Medicare, your recommended vaccines are now covered at 100%. Here's what that means for you:

- **No more high out-of-pocket costs** – If you need a Medicare-covered vaccine, it's free at the pharmacy or your doctor's office.
- **Better protection against serious diseases** – Shingles, pneumonia, and tetanus can all cause severe complications in older adults.
- **Lower risk of hospital stays** – Preventative vaccines help you stay out of the hospital, avoiding costly medical bills and serious illness.
- **Long-term health benefits** – A strong immune system means you get to enjoy a better quality of life as you age.

Why This Matters
Skipping vaccines can be life-threatening. Pneumonia alone hospitalizes over a million seniors each year, and shingles can cause painful nerve damage that lasts for months. By making these vaccines free, Medicare is ensuring that cost is no longer a barrier to essential healthcare.

What's Next?
This change is part of a bigger effort to make preventive care more accessible. If you haven't already, check with your doctor or pharmacy to make sure you're up to date on all your Medicare-covered vaccines. Staying protected is now easier—and free!

#3: Elimination of the Medicare Part D "Donut Hole"

If you've ever hit the Medicare Part D "Donut Hole," you know how frustrating—and expensive—it can be. This coverage gap left many seniors like you paying much higher out-of-pocket costs for their medications, making it even harder to afford prescriptions when they needed them most.

But starting in 2025, that's finally changing. The Inflation Reduction Act (IRA) is getting rid of the Donut Hole, so Medicare recipients will no longer face sudden cost increases once they reach a certain spending threshold.

Here's what that means for you:

- **No more unexpected price jumps** – You'll have a more predictable cost structure for prescription medications.
- **Lower out-of-pocket spending** – Instead of paying a higher percentage of drug costs after reaching the Donut Hole, Medicare will provide consistent coverage throughout the year.
- **Easier budgeting** – With costs spread more evenly, it'll be easier to plan for medication expenses.

Why This Change Matters

Before the IRA, seniors who hit the Donut Hole were forced to pay more out-of-pocket until they reached catastrophic coverage, where Medicare would finally take over the majority of costs. This system led to huge financial burdens, forcing many to skip doses or delay refills.

By eliminating this gap, Medicare is making prescription costs more manageable and predictable—helping you get the medications you need without financial stress.

What's Next?

This change goes into effect this year. Until then, be sure to review your Medicare Part D plan, so you know what to expect as this transition happens. With these improvements, getting your medications will be simpler and more affordable than ever.

#4: MEDICARE PART D OUT-OF-POCKET COST CAP

If you take expensive prescription medications, you know how quickly costs can add up. In the past, Medicare beneficiaries had to spend $8,000 out of pocket before reaching catastrophic coverage, where Medicare would cover most of the remaining drug costs. That's a huge financial burden—especially for seniors on fixed incomes.

Starting this year, the Inflation Reduction Act (IRA) introduces a new $2,000 annual cap on out-of-pocket prescription drug costs. This means that once you hit $2,000 in spending, you won't pay another cent for covered medications for the rest of the year—a massive relief for those with chronic conditions or high-cost prescriptions.

Here's what this change means for you:

- No more spending beyond $2,000 per year on prescription drugs.
- Savings of thousands of dollars annually for seniors who rely on expensive medications.
- More predictable and manageable healthcare costs—no more surprises.

What's the Catch?
While this is great news for Medicare beneficiaries, the cost burden is shifting to private insurance companies like Humana and UnitedHealthcare. Previously, Medicare

covered 80% of drug costs, but now, insurance providers are responsible for a large share.

To offset these costs, many Medicare Advantage Plans are making adjustments, including:

- Reducing or eliminating extra benefits like dental, vision, and gym memberships.
- Introducing new medical and prescription drug deductibles.
- Adjusting formularies means some medications may no longer be covered.

What's Next?

This change will take effect in 2025, so be sure to review your Medicare Part D or Medicare Advantage plan before then. Understanding how your plan is changing will help you avoid surprises and plan your healthcare costs wisely.

What Does This Mean for Medicare in 2026 and Beyond?

The Inflation Reduction Act (IRA) has brought some major cost-saving benefits for Medicare recipients, but those savings have to come from somewhere. Since insurance companies are now covering a larger share of prescription drug costs, they're expected to adjust their Medicare Advantage plans in 2026 to balance out the new financial landscape.

So, what does that mean for you?

Possible Medicare Changes in 2026:

- **Higher premiums** – Some insurers may raise costs to offset increased drug coverage expenses.
- **Fewer-covered medications** – Some prescriptions that were previously covered may be removed from plan formularies.
- **Reduced benefits** – Extras like dental, vision, hearing, over-the-counter (OTC) products, and wellness programs could be cut or scaled back.
- **New restrictions** – More plans may introduce prior authorizations or higher-tier drug pricing, requiring you to get approval before filling certain prescriptions.

How to Prepare for These Changes
Medicare beneficiaries should make an effort to stay informed and proactive as 2026 approaches. Here's what you can do:

- **Review your plan annually** – Check what's changing in your Medicare Advantage or Part D plan before enrollment season.
- **Compare options** – If your premiums or drug costs go up, consider switching to a more affordable plan.
- **Check your medications** – If your prescription is no longer covered, talk to your doctor about alternatives.

- **Be aware of benefit reductions** – If your plan drops vision, dental, or fitness perks, you may need supplemental coverage.

The Bottom Line

The cost cap on prescriptions and the elimination of the Donut Hole are big wins for seniors, but insurance companies are adjusting to these changes, too. Staying aware and prepared will help you navigate this transition and make the best healthcare decisions moving forward.

#5: The M3P Program

Starting in 2025, Medicare is introducing a new program to help seniors better manage their prescription drug costs. The Medicare Prescription Payment Plan (M3P) allows beneficiaries to spread out their medication payments over time instead of paying large, upfront costs all at once.

This is great news for those who rely on expensive medications or take multiple prescriptions each month. Instead of getting hit with a huge bill all at once, you'll have the option to pay in predictable monthly installments—making it easier to budget your healthcare expenses.

How M3P Works:

- **Breaks up prescription costs** – No more large lump-sum payments for high-cost medications.
- **Makes budgeting easier** – M3P runs on a

12-month cycle, and the balance must be paid at the end of the year.
- **Helps seniors stay on their medication** – Reduces the risk of skipping prescriptions due to high costs.
- **Applies to Medicare Part D enrollees** – If you have Medicare prescription drug coverage, you'll have the option to enroll.

Why This Matters

For many seniors, out-of-pocket drug expenses are one of the biggest financial burdens. If you take lifesaving medications, this program can help you avoid financial strain while staying on track with your treatment.

What's Next?

The M3P program launches in 2025. Your Part D provider will administer the M3P program. Call them directly to enroll. If you struggle with high prescription costs, this program could be a game-changer—so keep an eye out for updates!

FINAL THOUGHTS ON THE INFLATION REDUCTION ACT

The Inflation Reduction Act (IRA) is bringing the biggest Medicare changes in nearly 20 years, making prescription drugs more affordable and predictable for seniors. From the $35 insulin cap to the elimination of the Part D Donut

Hole and the new $2,000 out-of-pocket maximum, these updates will save seniors thousands of dollars each year.

However, these changes come with trade-offs. Since private insurance companies are now covering a larger share of drug costs, Medicare Advantage plans may see higher premiums, fewer covered medications, or reductions in extra benefits like dental, vision, and wellness perks.

How to Stay Prepared

- **Review your Medicare plan every year** – Costs and coverage can change.
- **Watch for changes in covered medications** – Some prescriptions may no longer be included.
- **Compare different plans** – If your premiums or benefits shift, you may want to switch plans.
- **Stay informed** – Medicare is evolving, and understanding these changes will help you make the best decisions.

As we move into 2026 and beyond, staying proactive and informed will ensure you get the best possible coverage without surprises. Medicare is changing—but with the right knowledge, you can navigate it with confidence.

CHAPTER 6

Traditional Medicare or The Cadillac Plan

When it comes to Medicare, choosing the right plan isn't just about coverage—it's about flexibility, cost savings, and long-term security. If you want the best plan that lets you see any doctor, anywhere, without restrictions, then Traditional Medicare with a Supplement (Medigap Plan G)—often called the Cadillac Plan—is your best option.

This plan gives you freedom from networks, no referrals, and near-total financial protection, making it the top choice for those who want predictability and peace of mind in their healthcare.

Medicare Parts A & B cover a lot, but they don't cover everything. This, unfortunately, leaves you with significant out-of-pocket costs. That's where a Medicare Supplement (Medigap) Plan comes in, filling the gaps and ensuring you're covered anywhere in the U.S.

In this chapter, we'll explore:

- How Traditional Medicare Works and Why It Requires Additional Coverage.
- Why is Plan G the most popular Medicare Supplement, and how does it compare to other options?
- What costs should be expected, and how does pricing vary by location and provider?
- How this plan benefits people living in multiple states.
- Why Open Enrollment is critical—if you miss it, you may lose your best chance to get into this plan without medical underwriting.

If you value freedom, security, and financial protection, keep reading—you'll see why the Cadillac Plan is the smartest choice for many Medicare beneficiaries. Let's start by looking at how traditional Medicare works.

HOW TRADITIONAL MEDICARE WORKS

As we covered in a previous chapter, Medicare Parts A & B serve as your primary insurance, covering hospital stays, doctor visits, and medical services. Part A covers the cost of your inpatient hospital care, skilled nursing facilities, hospice, and even some home health services. Part B covers outpatient care, doctor visits, and preventive services. Together, they form the foundation of Medicare—but they have major gaps that can leave you with hefty out-of-pocket expenses.

WHY TRADITIONAL MEDICARE ALONE ISN'T ENOUGH

While Medicare provides much needed coverage, it doesn't cover everything. Some of the significant issues you'll encounter include:

- **No out-of-pocket maximum:** You're responsible for 20% of all medical costs, no matter how high they get.
- **Costly coinsurance:** A simple doctor visit or medical treatment means you owe 20% of the bill.
- **No prescription drug coverage:** You'll need a separate Part D plan to cover medications.

THE SOLUTION: A MEDICARE SUPPLEMENT (MEDIGAP) PLAN

Fortunately, you don't have to deal with these issues if you choose a Medigap Plan. A Medicare Supplement Plan, or Medigap, fills these gaps, making costs predictable and manageable. This plan:

- Covers co-pays, deductibles, and coinsurance Medicare doesn't pay.
- Lets you see any doctor, anywhere in the U.S., with no network restrictions.

2025 Medigap Plans

Benefits	Plans Available to All Applicants									Medicare first eligible before 2020 only	
	PLAN A	PLAN B	PLAN D	PLAN G	PLAN K	PLAN L	PLAN M	PLAN N	PLAN C	PLAN F
Medicare Part A coinsurance and hospital coverage (up to an additional 365 days after Medicare benefits are used up)	✓	✓	✓	✓	✓	✓	✓	✓	✓	✓
Medicare Part B coinsurance or Copayment	✓	✓	✓	✓	50%	75%	✓	✓ copays apply	✓	✓
Blood (first three pints each year)	✓	✓	✓	✓	50%	75%	✓	✓	✓	✓
Part A hospice care coinsurance or copayment	✓	✓	✓	✓	50%	75%	✓	✓	✓	✓
Skilled nursing facility coinsurance			✓	✓	50%	75%	✓	✓	✓	✓
Medicare Part A deductible		✓	✓	✓	50%	75%	50%	✓	✓	✓
Medicare Part B deductible									✓	✓
Medicare Part B excess charges				✓						✓
Foreign travel emergency (up to plan limits)			✓	✓			✓	✓	✓	✓
Out-of-pocket limit in 2025					$7,220	$3,610				

Adapted from Medicare.gov © Christine Ames LLC

- Provides financial protection from overwhelming medical bills.

Without a Medigap plan, one major illness could cost thousands. That's why choosing the right supplement plan is essential to guarantee you're getting proper care without breaking the bank.

This chart provides an overview of all the Medicare Supplement Plans available. This is available in the Medicare and You Handbook. All Medicare Supplements are identical plans with the same coverage. If you look through your piles of mail, you will see this chart from AARP, Mutual of Omaha, Blue Cross Blue Shield, and others. The difference is simply price. Some will offer a discount for living with someone or a household discount if you and your spouse both have a plan. You can shop these plans by price with a local agent or on Medicare.gov.

Make note of the checkmarks. Some plans have more gaps that others. For example Plan A, has several check marks missing. Plan F is no longer for sale. Plan G has been it's replacement, with only one check mark missing, Part B Deductible.

MEDICARE SUPPLEMENT (MEDIGAP) PLANS: WHY PLAN G IS THE BEST CHOICE

Medicare Supplement (Medigap) plans help cover the out-of-pocket costs that Original Medicare leaves behind. Among these options, Plan G is the best and most comprehensive choice for new enrollees. However, there are other Medicare Supplement plan options to choose from:

- **Plan G:** The most popular plan, covering nearly all costs except the small Part B deductible ($257 per year).
- **Plan N:** Lower premiums but includes co-pays for doctor visits and potentially higher out-of-pocket expenses, excess charges not covered.
- **High Deductible Plan G (HDG):** A budget-friendly alternative with a lower monthly premium but a $2,870 annual deductible.

Why Plan G Stands Above the Rest

Before 2020, Plan F was the top option because it covered everything, but it had higher premiums and is no longer available for new enrollees. Plan G now offers the best balance of affordability and protection. Plan G stands out because of its benefits, making it the Cadillac Plan:

- **No networks:** See any doctor or specialist nationwide without restrictions.
- **No referrals or prior authorizations:** Get the care you need hassle-free.
- **Predictable costs:** With only a small annual deductible, there are no surprise medical bills.
- **Full financial protection:** Covers all Medicare-approved services after the deductible, eliminating major medical expenses.

If you're looking for total peace of mind and flexibility, Plan G is the superior choice for you. And best of all, all Plan G policies have the same coverage. It's like shopping at Walmart or Whole Foods—the pasta you buy will be the same, it's just a different store!

Plan G chart, also on Medicare.gov. Please notice the three columns: Medicare Pays, Plan G Pays, You Pay. You want to pay attention to "You Pay," as it mostly shows zeros. If you stay in the hospital for more than 365 days, you will be responsible for all associated costs. That is just not something that happens. A skilled nursing facility, as explained in Chapter 1, is a form of rehabilitation. Most people only stay for the first 20 days and then return home for home health care or to a nursing home. Your only real responsibility is the $257 annual deductible.

Plan G – Medicare Part A – Hospitals – Per Benefit Period

SERVICES	MEDICARE PAYS	PLAN G PAYS	YOU PAY
HOSPITALIZATION* Semiprivate room and board, general nursing, and miscellaneous services and supplies			
First 60 days	All but $1,676	$1,676 (Part A deductible)	$0
61st through 90th day	All but $419 a day	$419 a day	$0
91st day and after: While using 60 lifetime reserve days	All but $838 a day	$838 a day	$0
Once lifetime reserve days are used: Additional 365 days	$0	100% of Medicare-eligible expenses	$0**
Beyond the additional 365 days	$0	$0	All costs
SKILLED NURSING FACILITY CARE* You must meet Medicare's requirements, including having been in a hospital for at least 3 days and entered a Medicare-approved facility within 30 days after leaving the hospital			
First 20 days	All approved amounts	$0	$0
21st through 100th day	All but $209.50 a day	Up to $209.50 a day	$0
101st day and after	$0	$0	All costs
BLOOD			
First 3 pints	$0	3 pints	$0
Additional amounts	100%	$0	$0
HOSPICE CARE You must meet Medicare's requirements, including a doctor's certification of terminal illness	All but very limited copayment/coinsurance for outpatient drugs and inpatient respite care	Medicare copayment/coinsurance	$0

Adapted from Medicare.gov © Christine Ames LLC

Plan G – Medicare Part B – Doctors – Per Benefit Period

SERVICES	MEDICARE PAYS	PLAN G PAYS	YOU PAY
MEDICAL EXPENSES - IN OR OUT OF THE HOSPITAL AND OUTPATIENT HOSPITAL TREATMENT, such as physician's services, inpatient and outpatient medical and surgical services and supplies, physical and speech therapy, diagnostic tests, durable medical equipment			
First $257 of Medicare-approved amounts*	$0	$0	$257 (Part B deductible)
Remainder of Medicare-approved amounts	Generally 80%	Generally 20%	$0
Part B Excess Charges (above Medicare-approved amounts)			
You must meet Medicare's requirements, including having been in a hospital for at least 3 days and entered a Medicare-approved facility within 30 days after leaving the hospital			
First 20 days	$0	100%	$0
BLOOD			
First 3 pints	$0	All costs	$0
Next $257 of Medicare-approved amounts*	$0	$0	$257 (Part B deductible)
Remainder of Medicare-approved amounts	80%	20%	$0
CLINICAL LABORATORY SERVICES - TESTS FOR DIAGNOSTIC SERVICES	100%	$0	$0
PARTS A AND B			
HOME HEALTH CARE - MEDICARE-APPROVED SERVICES			
Medically necessary skilled care services and medical supplies	100%	$0	$0
DURABLE MEDICAL EQUIPMENT			
First $257 of Medicare-approved amounts*	$0	$0	$257 (Part B deductible)
Remainder of Medicare-approved amounts	80%	20%	$0

Adapted from Medicare.gov © Christine Ames LLC

HOW PRICING WORKS FOR MEDICARE SUPPLEMENTS

While Medicare Supplement (Medigap) Plan G offers the same coverage across all providers, the cost varies based on several factors. Understanding what affects pricing can help you find the best deal and save money.

There are a few factors that affect these supplement plans, including the following:

- **Zip code:** Medigap prices vary significantly by state and even county.
- Age at Enrollment: The younger you enroll, the lower your premium will be. Premiums increase with age.
- **Gender:** Women often pay less than men for the same coverage.
- **Smoking status:** Smokers typically face higher premiums.

To understand what the cost of Plan G could look like for you, let's look at an example. The average monthly premium for Plan G typically costs between $100-$300, but this all depends on your location. However, in Florida, the rates are nearly double the average in other states because of higher healthcare costs and increased claims.

How to Get the Best Rate

If you'd like to get the best rate, it is important not to settle for the first quote you receive. Here are some tips to help you find the best price possible for your Plan G:

- **Compare multiple companies:** Aetna, Cigna, Blue Cross Blue Sheild, United Health Care, and Mutual of Omaha and more all offer Plan G with identical coverage but different pricing.
- **Use an independent agent:** A knowledgeable agent can find the best price across different carriers.
- **Ask about discounts:** Some companies offer a "household" discount, which means either you and your spouse enjoy the same plan or a "living with someone" discount that can save you up to 25%.

Shopping around ensures you get the same great coverage at the lowest possible price. If nothing else, you can confirm that the first supplement plan you find is the best one available.

WHY TRADITIONAL MEDICARE IS BEST FOR MULTI-STATE RESIDENTS

If you live in multiple states throughout the year, Traditional Medicare with a Medicare Supplement (Medigap) Plan is the best option. Unlike Medicare Advantage plans, which

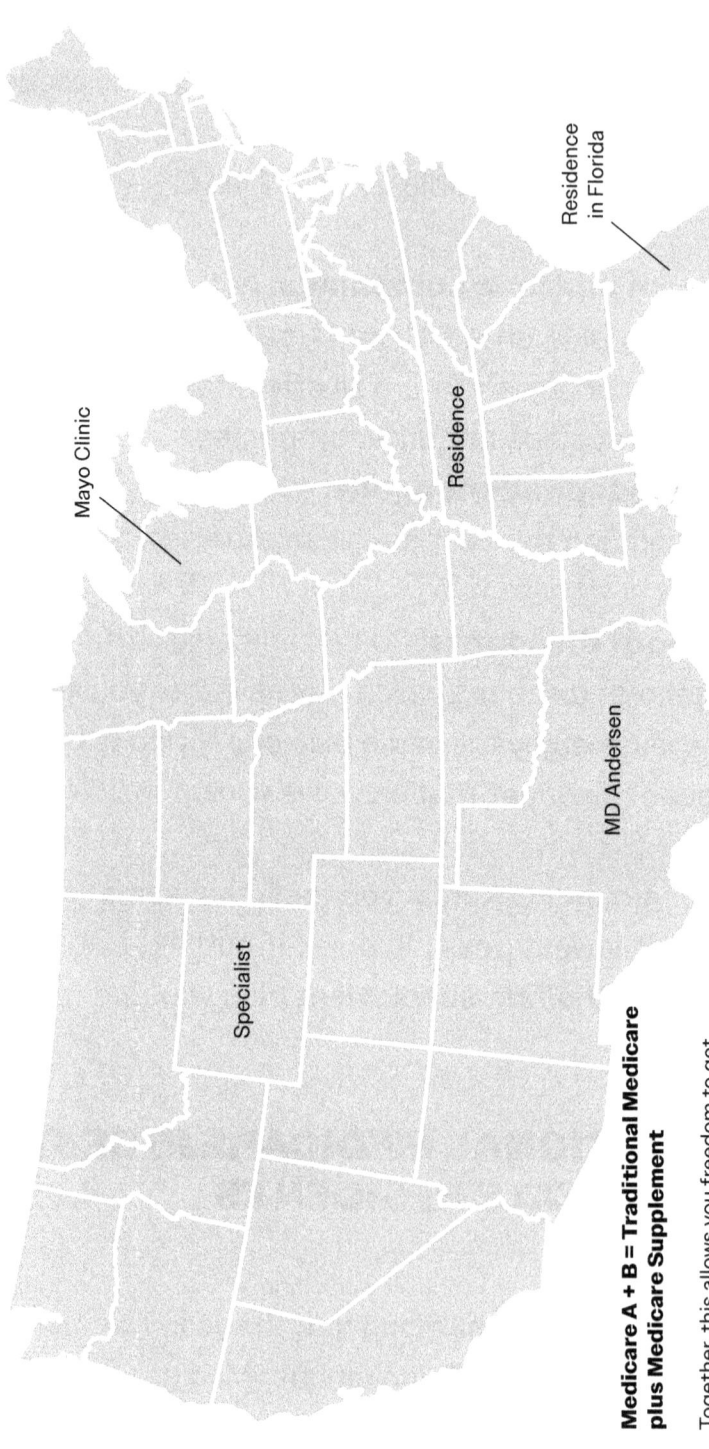

Medicare A + B = Traditional Medicare plus Medicare Supplement

Together, this allows you freedom to get care anywhere in the United States.
- No Networks
- No Prior Authorization
- No Restrictions

* Mayo Clinic and MD Anderson do not accept Medicare Advantage

have restricted networks, Traditional Medicare allows for a visit to any doctor anywhere in the U.S. as long as they accept Medicare.

Get Healthcare Anywhere You Live or Travel

If you spend winters in Florida and summers in Tennessee, this plan gives you seamless coverage across state lines. You can travel to and from your various residences without having to complete any paperwork or make any changes. You never have to switch networks or worry about losing access to your doctors when relocating seasonally.

Enjoy Nationwide Access to the Best Specialists

Additionally, you'll have access to some of the best medical facilities in the country: MD Anderson (Texas), Mayo Clinic, and Cleveland Clinic. They are fully covered under this plan. Best of all, there are no restrictions, which gives you the freedom to see top specialists without referrals.

No Need for Prior Authorizations

Unlike Medicare Advantage, which often requires pre-approvals for treatments, Traditional Medicare allows you to get care without delays. That means no insurance red tape! Simply show up for treatment and receive care.

As you can see, if you travel or reside in multiple states, Traditional Medicare eliminates hassles and ensures you have full, nationwide access to care.

PRESCRIPTION DRUG COVERAGE: THE ROLE OF PART D

While Traditional Medicare (Parts A & B) covers hospital and medical services, it does not include prescription drug coverage. To fill this gap, you need a Medicare Part D plan, which provides standalone drug coverage and helps lower medication costs.

Medicare Part D Explained

Medicare Part D is required if you want prescription drug coverage under Traditional Medicare. These plans are offered by numerous private insurance companies that Medicare has approved. In 2022, the average monthly premium was $33.37. In 2023, this rose to $31.50. In 2024, it was $42, and this year, in 2025, it is $45.

What to Expect for Annual Deductibles & Costs

Part D plans possess an annual deductible that increases yearly (varies by plan). In 2022, the Part D deductible was $480, rising to $505 in 2023 and $545 in 2024. In 2025, that deductible is now $615. However, starting in 2025, a new rule from the Inflation Reduction Act caps out-of-pocket costs at $2,000 annually, ensuring that no one on Medicare pays beyond that limit.

Why You Must Compare Plans Annually

You might think that you can just select a plan and stick

with it. However, like other insurance plans, you'll need to compare your plan annually to see if you're getting the best value and what you require to support your health.

Additionally, drug formularies change every year, meaning a medication that was covered this year may not be covered next year. Some plans also drop certain medications or shift them to a higher-cost tier. If you work with a good agent, they should review and adjust your Part D plan each year to ensure you're not overpaying or stuck with unexpected out-of-pocket costs.

EMERGENCY & TRAVEL COVERAGE UNDER TRADITIONAL MEDICARE

One of the most significant advantages of Traditional Medicare with a Medicare Supplement (Medigap) Plan is its nationwide emergency coverage. Unlike Medicare Advantage, which often limits coverage to a specific network, Traditional Medicare ensures you're protected anywhere in the U.S.

International Travel: Limited Coverage

Unfortunately, Medicare does not fully cover medical emergencies outside the U.S. Some Medicare Supplement (Medigap) plans offer a small foreign travel emergency benefit, but it only covers up to $50,000 and requires a 20% coinsurance.

If you experience a serious international medical emergency (like a hospital stay or medical evacuation), this can cost tens of thousands of dollars. If you plan to travel internationally, always get travel insurance to ensure full protection from unexpected medical expenses.

COST BREAKDOWN: WHAT YOU CAN EXPECT TO PAY FOR MEDIGAP

Understanding the actual cost of Traditional Medicare with a Supplement (Medigap Plan) is crucial when planning your healthcare budget. While this option provides comprehensive coverage and financial security, it does come with monthly premiums and some out-of-pocket costs.

With the Traditional Medicare route you will have three separate cards. Your Medicare Care Card and your Medicare Supplement Card you present to doctors and hospitals. Your stand alone prescription drug card is for pharmacies. Please note that these images are intended as examples. To demonstrate appearance and labels, and in no way an endorsement of any company. You can see the Supplement Card labeled with the Plan G chosen. The stand alone Prescription Drug Card is labeled as such. It may also be labeled as PDP for Prescription Drug Plan.

MEDICARE HEALTH INSURANCE

Name/Nombre
CHRISTINE AMES

Medicare Number/Numero de Medicare
1EG4-TE5-MK72

Entitled to/Con derecho a
HOSPITAL (PART A)
MEDICAL (PART B)

Coverage starts/Cobertura empieza
03-01-2025
03-01-2025

Insurance ID Card

ABC Health Insurance Company

Christine Ames
Policy Number: XXXXXX
Medicare Supplement Plan G
Policyholder Since 04/2025

Member USA Senior Care Network

Medicare Prescription Drug Plans

Name: Christine Ames

Customer ID: XXXXXX
Health Plan (80840) 9151014609
RxBIN: 017010
RxPCN: CIMCARE
RxGroup: CIGPDPRX

MedicareRx
Prescription Drug Coverage

S5617_<PBP>

Estimated Monthly Premiums (Based on Middle America Pricing)

- **Medicare Part A:** $0 (Most people qualify for free Part A based on work history.)
- **Medicare Part B:** $185 per month
- **Medicare Supplement Plan G:** $150 per month (Cost varies by state.)
- **Medicare Part D (Prescription Drug Plan):** $7 - $125 per month, depending on coverage.
- **Total Estimated Cost:** $300 - $400 per month

If you live in Florida, New York, or California, Medicare Supplement Plan G premiums can be as high as $400 per month, but Iowa and Nebraska's premiums may be as low as $100 on average.

Out-of-Pocket Costs: What You'll Actually Pay

- Plan G covers everything except the Medicare Part B deductible.
- Annual Part B deductible: $257 per year (after that, Medicare and Plan G cover 100% of approved costs).
- No co-pays, no coinsurance, and no unexpected medical bills—just predictable, manageable expenses.

This means for $300 - $400 per month, you get nationwide access to care, no networks, no referrals, and financial peace of mind. Compared to unpredictable costs with Medicare Advantage, this is a superior option for those who want total control over their healthcare.

THE CRITICAL OPEN ENROLLMENT WINDOW

Regarding Medicare enrollment, timing is essential. If you're approaching age 65, your Open Enrollment Period is the best time to secure the most comprehensive coverage with zero restrictions. Missing this window can limit your options and increase costs later.

Why Turning 65 Is the Best Time to Enroll

During your Medicare Open Enrollment Period (three months before the month you turn 65 and three months after you turn 65 then enroll in Part B), you get guaranteed approval for a Medicare Supplement (Medigap) Plan—no medical questions asked.

If you miss this window, you may have to undergo medical underwriting if you want a Medicare Supplement later. Pre-existing conditions may lead to even higher premiums or a denial of coverage.

Fortunately, if you miss Open Enrollment at 65, you may still qualify under Guaranteed Issue Rights—for example, if you lose employer coverage or leave a Medicare Advantage plan within your first year. However, your plan choices may be limited, and pricing may be higher.

More details on Open Enrollment are in Chapter 9.

FINAL THOUGHTS ON TRADITIONAL MEDICARE/THE CADILLAC PLAN

Choosing the right Medicare plan is one of the most important financial decisions you'll ever make. If you want maximum coverage, no restrictions, and financial peace of mind, Traditional Medicare with Plan G is the Cadillac Plan—offering the best flexibility and protection against medical costs.

Moving forward, it's time to get quotes from multiple companies, as prices will vary for identical coverage. Don't forget to enroll in Medicare Part D to avoid late penalties. If you're turning 65, enroll NOW—Open Enrollment is your best chance for guaranteed coverage.

The right Medicare plan gives you peace of mind, financial security, and freedom. Take action today and lock in the best coverage before it's too late.

CHAPTER 7

Medicare Advantage Pros and Cons

Medicare Advantage—or Medicare Part C—is a private insurance alternative to Original Medicare. It combines hospital, medical, and often prescription drug coverage into a single plan, simplifying healthcare for many seniors. While some people love the convenience and cost savings, others find the trade-offs—like provider restrictions—too limiting.

Before signing up, it's important to weigh the pros and cons. Can you live with a limited doctor network? Are the lower monthly costs worth potentially higher expenses when you need care? Medicare Advantage isn't one-size-fits-all, so take time to compare plans carefully.

Now, let's break down how Medicare Advantage works and whether it's the right choice for you.

WHAT IS MEDICARE ADVANTAGE?

Medicare Advantage, or Part C, is a private insurance plan that works with Medicare. These plans must follow federal regulations but are managed by private insurers, not the government. Instead of juggling separate Medicare Part A (hospital insurance) and Part B (medical insurance) cards, enrollees get one card that covers everything.

Think of it like employer-based health insurance. The insurance company, not Medicare, handles claims, sets network rules, and determines which doctors and hospitals you can see. Most plans bundle hospital, medical, and prescription drug coverage into one, making things simple.

Many people like Medicare Advantage for its convenience and extra benefits, such as dental and vision coverage. But there are trade-offs. These plans often have provider restrictions, may require referrals for specialists, and can come with unexpected out-of-pocket costs. Understanding these limitations is key before enrolling.

KEY FEATURES OF MEDICARE ADVANTAGE PLANS

Medicare Advantage plans always include Medicare Part A (hospital insurance) and Part B (medical insurance), covering essential healthcare needs like hospital stays, doctor visits, and outpatient care.

A major perk of Medicare Advantage is that most plans also include Medicare Part D, which covers prescription drugs. This eliminates the hassle of signing up for a separate drug plan, making healthcare management much simpler. Instead of juggling multiple cards and providers, enrollees get one plan, one card, and one insurer handling everything.

GOLD PLUS (HMO)
A Medicare Health Plan with Prescription Drug Coverage

See Back for Dental   CARD ISSUED: MM/DD/YY

CHRISTINE AMES
Member ID: HXXXXXXXX
Plan (80840) 91461101
RxBIN: XXXXXX
RxPCN: XXXXXXXX
RxGRP: XXXXX

MedicareR_x
Prescription Drug Coverage
CMS XXXXX XXX

Another reason Medicare Advantage is attractive? Extra benefits that Original Medicare doesn't cover. Depending on the plan, you might get:

- Dental coverage for cleanings, fillings, and dentures.
- Vision care, including eye exams, glasses, and contacts.
- Hearing aid discounts or allowances.
- Gym memberships, like SilverSneakers.
- Monthly allowances for over-the-counter (OTC) medications and wellness products.
- Healthy food cards with grocery funds.

These perks vary by plan and location, so comparing options carefully and ensuring your specific healthcare needs are covered before enrolling is important.

WHO BENEFITS THE MOST FROM MEDICARE ADVANTAGE?

Medicare Advantage may be a great option for some people, but it's not the best fit for everyone. Understanding who benefits the most can help determine if this plan aligns with your healthcare needs.

Where You Live Matters

Your location plays a huge role in the quality and availability of Medicare Advantage plans.

- **Urban areas:** If you live in a city, you'll likely have multiple plans with strong provider networks, extra benefits, and lower costs.
- **Rural areas:** Medicare Advantage plans are often limited, with fewer doctors and hospitals in-network. Copays and out-of-pocket costs may also be higher. If you're in a rural area, always check if your doctors accept the plan before enrolling.

Lower Monthly Premiums vs. Higher Costs When You Need Care

Many choose Medicare Advantage because some plans

have low or even $0 monthly premiums. However, this comes with a trade-off.

- You'll pay more out-of-pocket when you need medical care through copays, deductibles, and coinsurance.
- This could be a good fit if you're generally healthy and don't visit doctors often.
- Your out-of-pocket costs could
- add up quickly if you need frequent care or specialized treatment.

Comfortable with Network Restrictions?

Medicare Advantage works like an employer-sponsored health plan, meaning:

- HMO plans require you to see in-network doctors and get referrals for specialists.
- PPO plans allow more flexibility but charge higher costs if you go out-of-network.

If you prioritize lower monthly premiums and don't mind sticking to a network, Medicare Advantage may be a good choice. Always confirm your preferred doctors and hospitals accept the plan before signing up.

MEDICARE ADVANTAGE PLAN TYPES

When choosing a Medicare Advantage plan, it's important to understand the two primary options available: Health Maintenance Organization (HMO) plans and Preferred Provider Organization (PPO) plans. Each has advantages and limitations, so the best choice depends on your healthcare needs and preferences.

Health Maintenance Organization (HMO) Plans

HMO plans are typically the most affordable but come with strict provider network rules:

- **Primary Care Physician (PCP) Required:** You must select a PCP to coordinate your care and provide referrals for specialists.
- **Lower Monthly Costs:** HMOs usually offer lower premiums, copays, and out-of-pocket expenses than PPOs.
- **Limited Out-of-Network Coverage:** Unless it's an emergency, you must use in-network doctors and hospitals, or you'll have to pay the full cost of care.

Preferred Provider Organization (PPO) Plans

PPO plans offer more flexibility, but that freedom comes at a cost:

- **No PCP or Referrals Required:** You can see specialists directly without needing a referral.
- **In-Network vs. Out-of-Network:** You can go out of network, but you'll pay more for care—and some services may not be covered at all.
- **Major Limitation:** Some top hospitals like MD Anderson and Mayo Clinic do not accept Medicare Advantage PPOs.

Which Plan is Right for You?

If lower costs and a structured provider network are most important, an HMO may be your best bet. However, if you want more provider flexibility and don't mind higher costs, a PPO might be the better fit.

Before enrolling, always check if your preferred doctors and hospitals accept the plan!

KEY CONSIDERATIONS BEFORE CHOOSING MEDICARE ADVANTAGE

Medicare Advantage plans offer a convenient, all-in-one alternative to Original Medicare, but not all plans are the same. Before enrolling, carefully evaluate these four key factors to ensure the plan meets your healthcare needs.

1. Provider Network: Are Your Doctors Covered?

One of the biggest downsides of Medicare Advantage is restricted provider networks. Some doctors, hospitals, and specialists may not accept your plan, which could force you to switch providers or pay out-of-pocket.

Action Step: Before enrolling, confirm that your primary care doctor, specialists, and preferred hospital are in-network. If not, consider a plan with better provider access.

2. Prescription Drug Coverage: Check the Plan's Formulary

Many Medicare Advantage plans include prescription drug coverage (Part D), but not all medications are covered, and some may be placed in higher-cost tiers.

Action Step: Check the plan's formulary to see if your prescriptions are covered and at what cost. If you take regular medications, this step could save you hundreds each year.

3. Travel & Emergency Coverage: Know the Limits

- Emergency care is covered nationwide, but you must go to an ER to get full coverage.
- Urgent care outside your home state may not be covered, leaving you with unexpected costs.
- International travel is not covered. If you travel abroad, you will need separate travel insurance.

Action Step: If you travel often, confirm how your plan handles out-of-state care or consider a more flexible option.

4. Cost Considerations: Out-of-Pocket Expenses Add Up

Even if a plan has a low or $0 monthly premium, you could face high out-of-pocket expenses when you need care.

- **Medicare Part B Premium:** You must still pay your Part B premium ($185/month, this amount goes up annually).
- **Max Out-of-Pocket (MOOP):** Each plan sets an annual spending cap, which is crucial for those managing serious conditions like cancer.
- **Copays & Cost-Sharing:**
    - Specialist visits can have high copays.
    - Hospital stays may lead to hefty bills.
    - MRIs and CT scans often come with unexpected costs.

Do Your Research Before You Enroll

Medicare Advantage can be a great option, but only if it fits your unique healthcare needs. Take the time to compare provider networks, prescription coverage, and costs before enrolling. A well-researched decision today can save you money and frustration down the road.

THE DRAW OF EXTRA BENEFITS

One of the biggest selling points of Medicare Advantage plans is the extra benefits they offer—perks that Original

Medicare does not cover. While these additions can be attractive, they should never be the primary reason for choosing a plan. Your provider network, out-of-pocket costs, and overall coverage should always take priority.

Common Extra Benefits in Medicare Advantage Plans

Many Medicare Advantage plans offer additional benefits, such as:

- **Dental Coverage:** Includes routine cleanings, dentures, and sometimes implants.
- **Vision Care:** Covers eye exams, glasses, and contact lenses.
- **Hearing Aids:** Offers discounts or allowances for hearing devices.
- **Health & Wellness Perks:** Includes gym memberships, transportation assistance, and OTC allowances.
- **Food & Grocery Allowances:** Monthly stipends for nutritious food purchases.

Important Considerations

Before enrolling based on these benefits, remember:

- Availability varies—not all plans offer the same perks.
- Benefits can change yearly—what's covered this year may not be covered next year.

- Network and costs matter more—perks won't help if your preferred doctors aren't included in the plan.

Focus on Core Coverage First

While extra benefits are a nice addition, the real value of a Medicare Advantage plan lies in its medical coverage and affordability. Choose a plan based on your healthcare needs, and view perks as a bonus rather than the deciding factor.

PROS AND CONS OF MEDICARE ADVANTAGE

Medicare Advantage plans provide an alternative to Original Medicare by bundling multiple types of coverage into a single plan. While they can help lower costs and offer additional benefits, they also come with limitations. Weighing the pros and cons carefully will help you determine whether this option aligns with your healthcare needs.

Pros of Medicare Advantage

- **Lower Monthly Premiums:** Many Medicare Advantage plans come with low or even $0 additional monthly premiums beyond the standard Part B premium, making them a budget-friendly option for many seniors.
- **All-in-One Convenience:** Instead of managing separate plans for hospital, medical, and

prescription drug coverage, Medicare Advantage consolidates everything into a single plan with one card.
- **Extra Benefits:** Many plans offer additional perks not covered by Original Medicare, such as dental, vision, hearing aids, wellness programs, and even grocery or over-the-counter allowances.
- **Out-of-Pocket Protection:** Unlike Original Medicare, which has no spending cap, Medicare Advantage plans set a maximum out-of-pocket (MOOP) limit each year, helping protect against catastrophic medical costs.

Cons of Medicare Advantage

- **Limited Provider Networks:** Many plans require you to use in-network doctors and hospitals, meaning you may need to switch providers.
- **Higher Out-of-Pocket Costs:** While premiums are lower, costs can add up quickly through copays, deductibles, and coinsurance when receiving care.
- **Restrictions for Travelers:** If you frequently travel or live in multiple states, you may face challenges getting non-emergency care outside your plan's coverage area.
- **No International Coverage:** Unlike some Medigap plans, Medicare Advantage does not cover medical expenses outside the U.S.

Weighing Your Options

Medicare Advantage can be a great choice for those prioritizing lower premiums and extra benefits, but it's important to consider the potential trade-offs. Be sure to compare your healthcare needs, preferred doctors, and travel habits before making your decision.

MAKING AN INFORMED DECISION

Choosing a Medicare Advantage plan is all about making sure the plan fits your healthcare needs and budget. While these plans offer potential savings and extra benefits, they also come with network restrictions and varying out-of-pocket costs. Taking time to evaluate your options now can help you avoid costly surprises later.

Assess Your Needs

Start by asking yourself a few key questions:

- Do you need access to a broad network of doctors, or are you comfortable with limited provider choices?
- How often do you travel outside your home state? Will network restrictions impact your ability to receive care?
- Can you manage higher copays and out-of-pocket costs in exchange for lower monthly premiums?

Compare Plans in Your Area

Medicare Advantage plan quality and affordability vary by location. If you live in a metro area, you may have more options, lower costs, and broader networks. Rural residents, however, may face higher expenses and fewer provider choices.

Work with an Expert

A local Medicare agent can help you compare plans, confirm that your preferred doctors and hospitals are covered, and break down out-of-pocket costs, including copays and maximum spending limits.

THE BOTTOM LINE: DO YOUR RESEARCH BEFORE YOU MAKE YOUR CHOICE

Medicare Advantage offers lower monthly costs and extra benefits like dental, vision, and prescription coverage. However, it also comes with trade-offs—limited provider networks, potential high out-of-pocket costs, and restrictions on out-of-state care.

Before enrolling, compare plans, review costs, and confirm that your doctors accept the plan. A licensed Medicare agent can help you navigate the options and avoid unexpected expenses.

Making an informed decision now ensures you get the right coverage without surprises later. Take your time, ask questions, and choose a plan that truly fits your healthcare needs.

CHAPTER 8

Common Rookie Mistakes to Avoid

When navigating Medicare, it's easy to fall into common traps that can lead you to unexpected costs, coverage gaps, or regret. Below are people's most frequent mistakes—and how to avoid them.

1. FALLING FOR CALL CENTER SALES PITCHES

Medicare call centers operate as sales-driven businesses, not personalized advisors. Their goal is to enroll you in Medicare Advantage, not to ensure you get the best coverage for your healthcare needs. These agents talk fast, often rushing you into a decision without verifying whether your doctors are in-network or if your medications are covered.

This aggressive sales approach is most common during the Annual Enrollment Period (AEP) when many seniors switch plans. What they don't tell you is that you can submit multiple applications during AEP, but only the last one processed takes effect. This means if you enroll in a plan early in the period, but later get talked into a different one by a pushy call center agent, the second plan will override your previous choice—potentially leaving you with coverage that doesn't suit your needs.

Solution:

Instead of relying on commission-driven call centers, work with a local, independent Medicare agent who will take the time to review your doctors, hospitals, and medications—ensuring your plan truly fits your healthcare needs.

2. NOT CHOOSING A LOCAL AGENT

Not all Medicare agents provide the same level of service. While a good agent will take the time to compare your options, look up your doctors and medications, and provide ongoing support.

A seasoned local agent—with at least five years of experience—understands the hospital networks in your area and will help you compare Medicare Advantage, Medicare Supplement, and stand-alone Part D drug plans. If an agent sells you a Medicare Supplement but refuses to assist with a drug plan, that's a red flag. A reliable agent should help with all aspects of your Medicare coverage.

Additionally, good agents answer their phones and

communicate with their clients. While it's natural for them to get busy during Annual Enrollment, they should still be responsive and available when you have questions.

Solution:
Before choosing an agent, ask friends and family for referrals and seek out someone who is communicative, knowledgeable, and willing to provide full Medicare support.

3. FALLING FOR FOOD CARD GIMMICKS

If you've watched daytime TV, you've probably seen commercials promising "$3,600 in annual food benefits" for Medicare enrollees. While this sounds like a great deal, the reality is that very few people qualify for the maximum amount. These ads are designed to get you to call—not to ensure you get the proper coverage.

Who Actually Qualifies?

- Large food card allowances (such as the $3,600 benefit) are only available to Dual-Eligible beneficiaries—those who have both Medicare and Medicaid and live below the poverty level.
- Some Chronic Special Needs Plans (CSNPs) offer food card benefits for those with diabetes, heart disease, or COPD, but these typically range from $50 to $75 per month.

- Food cards have become more common due to inflation, but they should never be the primary reason for choosing a plan.

Solution:

Before enrolling, verify eligibility and ensure the plan meets your core healthcare needs. Never select a Medicare plan based solely on extra perks like food cards

4. MISUNDERSTANDING THE PART B GIVE BACK PROGRAM

A Medicare Advantage Give Back Plan can seem like a great deal—it reduces your Medicare Part B premium, putting more money back into your Social Security check each month. However, many people don't realize the trade-offs involved.

How Does It Work?

- Anyone enrolled in Medicare Advantage can qualify for a Give Back plan—there are no income restrictions or eligibility requirements.
- The amount varies by location—larger cities tend to offer higher Give Back amounts.
- Example: If a plan provides a $100 Give Back, your monthly Part B cost drops from $185 to $85.

The Trade-Off: What You Give Up

While a Give Back plan puts money back into your pocket, it cuts back on other benefits in return. Many plans reduce or eliminate:

- Higher copays for specialists and overnight in the hospital
- Higher max out of pocket
- Dental, vision, and hearing benefits
- Over-the-counter (OTC) allowances
- Healthy food cards
- Gym memberships (like SilverSneakers)

Solution:

If you rarely use extra benefits and prefer more cash flow, a Give Back plan may be worth considering. However, if you rely on dental, vision, or wellness perks, it's important to weigh whether the trade-off is worth it for your needs.

5. IGNORING CHRONIC ILLNESS CONSIDERATIONS

If you have a chronic illness such as diabetes, heart disease, or COPD, your healthcare needs will likely be higher than average. This means you'll require more frequent specialist visits, lab tests, and treatments, which can lead to higher medical expenses. Choosing the wrong Medicare plan could result in unexpected out-of-pocket costs or limited provider options when you need care the most.

Which Plan is Best for Chronic Conditions?

- **Medicare Advantage Special Needs Plans (CSNPs):** Some Medicare Advantage plans are specifically designed for individuals with chronic illnesses, offering disease-specific benefits such as lower copays for specialist visits, care coordination, and medication support.
- **Medicare Supplement (Medigap):** If affordable, a Medigap plan is often the best choice because it eliminates most out-of-pocket costs and allows nationwide access to doctors and specialists without network restrictions.

Solution:

If you have a chronic condition and can afford a Medicare Supplement plan, it's worth serious consideration. The predictable costs and broader provider access can save you money and ensure quality care over time. Compare all options carefully before making your decision.

6. ASSUMING YOU CAN KEEP YOUR ACA PLAN

Some people believe they can continue their Affordable Care Act (ACA) plan after turning 65 instead of enrolling in Medicare. This is a costly mistake that can leave you without health coverage for months.

What Happens When You Turn 65?

- The ACA is subsidized by the government based on income, but once you become Medicare-eligible, you are no longer eligible for those subsidies.
- If you are enrolled in Medicare Part A, your ACA plan will automatically drop you—but often AFTER your Medicare Open Enrollment has ended.
- This means you could lose health insurance entirely and have to wait until the next enrollment period to sign up for Medicare.

Why Can't You Stay on ACA?

- Federal rules prohibit people from being enrolled in both an ACA plan and Medicare.
- If you delay enrolling in Medicare, you could face penalties and be left without any coverage until the next enrollment window.

Solution:

To avoid coverage gaps and potential penalties, enroll in Medicare on time. If you're unsure about the transition, seek guidance from a local Medicare agent before your 65th birthday.

7. THINKING MEDICARE COVERS LONG-TERM CARE

Many people mistakenly think that Medicare also covers long-term care, but later, they face unexpected costs when they or a loved one require extended assistance. Medicare does not pay for custodial care, assisted living, memory care, or nursing homes.

What Does Medicare Cover?

- Short-term rehabilitation within a skilled nursing facility after a hospital stay.
- Therapy and medical support designed to help you regain independence after an illness, surgery, or injury.

What Medicare Does NOT Cover:

- **Custodial Care:** Assistance with daily activities including bathing, dressing, and eating.
- **Long-term Care Services:** Ongoing care for chronic conditions that require extended support like cognitive impairment.
- **Assisted living and nursing homes:** Unless short term medical rehabilitation is required, this is generally 20 days.

It's easy to see why this is confusing—Medicare may cover a short-term stay in a nursing home for rehab, but not long-term residency.

Solution:
To cover long-term care costs, you'll need private savings, Medicaid, or a Long Term Care Insurance policy. Planning ahead is a must to ensure you have the financial resources to cover extended care when needed.

8. MISUNDERSTANDING HOSPICE COVERAGE

Hospice care offers comfort and support for those facing a terminal illness, and Medicare fully covers hospice services. However, many people don't realize that room and board at a hospice facility are not included.

What Medicare Covers:

- Hospice care at home, which includes medications, medical equipment, and professional caregiver support.
- Pain management and symptom relief to improve quality of life.

What Medicare Does NOT Cover:

- Room and board at a hospice facility. If you opt to receive care in a hospice house or inpatient facility, you will likely have to pay daily room and board fees out-of-pocket.

Many families opt for at-home hospice care with the support of loved ones, as this is fully covered by Medicare.

Solution:

If considering a hospice facility, be sure to ask about costs upfront and plan accordingly to avoid unexpected expenses.

9. NOT ENROLLING IN PART D ON TIME

Many people skip enrolling in Medicare Part D (prescription drug coverage) because they don't currently take medications. However, delaying enrollment can lead to lifetime penalties and higher costs down the road.

Why You Must Enroll in Part D Immediately

- Even if you don't take prescriptions now, you must enroll in Part D when first eligible unless you have Creditable Coverage (like employer or VA coverage).
- Low-cost plans are available to ensure you have coverage without breaking the bank.

The Costly Late Enrollment Penalty

- Medicare enforces a 1% penalty for every month you go without Part D or Creditable Coverage.
- Example: If you delay enrollment for 5 years (60 months), your Part D premium permanently increases by 60%—for life.

Solution:

To avoid penalties, always enroll in a Part D plan when first eligible or ensure you have Creditable Coverage from an employer or the VA. Use Medicare.gov to compare plans in your area and find affordable options.

10. FAILING TO GET EMPLOYER CREDITABLE COVERAGE DOCUMENTATION

If you're delaying Medicare because you have employer-sponsored insurance, you must ensure your coverage is Creditable Coverage—meaning it meets Medicare's minimum standards.

Without Creditable Coverage, you could face late enrollment penalties for Part B and Part D, leading to higher costs for life.

Solution:

Before delaying Medicare, request written proof of Creditable Coverage from your employer. This documentation will protect you from penalties and ensure a smooth transition when you do enroll in Medicare. Always verify your coverage status to avoid unexpected financial consequences.

11. RELYING ONLY ON MEDICARE A & B (WITHOUT ADDITIONAL COVERAGE)

Some people assume Medicare Part A and Part B provide enough coverage, but this can lead to huge financial risks.

Why Medicare A & B Alone Isn't Enough:

- Part A (hospital coverage) has high deductibles for each hospital stay.
- Part B (medical coverage) requires you to pay 20% of all outpatient costs—with NO cap on how much you could owe.
  - 20% of open-heart surgery? A massive, unaffordable bill.
  - 20% of a simple doctor's visit? Manageable—but costs add up over time.

Without additional coverage, you are financially exposed to high medical expenses.

Solution:

To protect yourself, enroll in either a Medicare Supplement (Medigap) plan for low out-of-pocket costs or a Medicare Advantage plan for structured coverage with maximum spending limits. Ignoring this step could result in overwhelming medical bills.

12. NOT CHECKING DOCTOR & MEDICATION COVERAGE

One of the most common Medicare mistakes is failing to verify whether your doctors and medications are covered before enrolling in a plan. This oversight can lead to unexpected costs, denied prescriptions, or losing access to preferred providers.

Key Considerations Before Enrolling:

- Medicare Advantage plans have provider networks, meaning your doctor may not be in-network—which could result in higher out-of-pocket costs or needing to switch doctors.
- Medications are placed into pricing "tiers", and some may be expensive or not covered at all. If your medication isn't included in a plan's formulary, you may have limited options.

What to Do Before Enrolling:

- A local Medicare agent should check your doctors, hospitals, and medications before enrolling you in a plan.
- If a prescription drug isn't covered, explore options like a Formulary Exception or switching to an alternative medication.
- If enrolling in Traditional Medicare with a Supplement, your agent should also help you select a Part D drug plan to ensure your medications are covered.

Solution:

Always verify provider networks and drug coverage before choosing a plan. If an agent doesn't offer this service, move on and find one who does.

FINAL THOUGHTS

Avoiding these common Medicare mistakes can save you time, money, and frustration in the long run. Making the wrong decision could lead to unexpected costs, coverage gaps, or limited access to doctors and medications.

Take the time to research your options, compare plans carefully, and seek professional guidance from a trusted Medicare agent. A well-informed decision now ensures better coverage, financial protection, plus your peace of mind regarding your healthcare needs in the years ahead.

CHAPTER 9

Turning 65 and Open Enrollment

Turning 65 isn't just another birthday—it's a turning point in your healthcare journey. For many, this milestone marks the first time you're eligible for Medicare, and with that comes an opportunity that shouldn't be overlooked: your personal Medicare Open Enrollment Period or IEP.

Unlike the annual Medicare enrollment period you hear about on TV each fall, this one is just for you, and it only happens once. It's your chance to make decisions that can shape not only your coverage—but your peace of mind—for years to come.

What makes this window so important? During this time, you have access to coverage that, under any other circumstance, may be out of reach. You can choose a Medicare Supplement plan—often considered the gold standard of Medicare coverage—without answering a single medical question. No health screenings. No underwriting. No worry about being denied due to existing conditions.

But here's where many people go wrong: they confuse this once-in-a-lifetime enrollment window with the Annual Enrollment Period that happens every October through December. It's an easy mistake—especially if you're coming from an employer plan and used to making benefit choices at the end of each year. However, missing this window—or misunderstanding it—can limit your options later and lead to unexpected out-of-pocket costs.

This chapter will walk you through everything you need to know about your Turning 65 Open Enrollment Period—what it is, how it works, and why acting at the right time could be one of the most important decisions you make in retirement.

Let's make sure you don't miss the window—and don't miss the benefits you're entitled to.

WHAT IS OPEN ENROLLMENT?

When you're turning 65, Medicare gives you a special window of time to enroll in coverage—this is also known as your Initial Enrollment Period (IEP), often referred to as Open Enrollment for those new to Medicare.

This enrollment window spans seven months in total:

- Three months before your 65th birthday month
- Your birthday month
- Three months after your birthday month

7 Months to Enroll
Initial Election Period / Open Enrollment

Month 1	Month 2	Month 3	Month 4	Month 5	Month 6	Month 7
			Month you turn 65			

* Part A will start on the 1st day of your birth month

Sign Up Month	Your Part B Starts
Month 1, 2, 3	1st day of your birth month
Month 4, 5, 6, 7	1st day of next month

* Part B start date will always be 1st of the month
* If you enroll on May 4th your Part B will start June 1

© Copyright 2025 by Christine Ames and Christine Ames, LLC

During this time, you can enroll in Medicare Part A and Part B, and you have the freedom to choose the type of coverage that fits your needs. It's your chance to get started on the right foot—whether that means a Medicare Supplement plan or Medicare Advantage.

It's important not to confuse this with the Annual Enrollment Period, which is always from October 15 to December 7 and applies to people already on Medicare. For enrollment steps, refer back to Chapter 4 for full instructions on how to apply.

WHY YOU MUST START EARLY

Timing is everything when it comes to Medicare—and starting early can save you unnecessary stress, delays, and potential gaps in coverage. One of the biggest roadblocks people face is getting their Medicare Claim Number, which is required before you can enroll in a plan. This number comes from the Social Security Administration, and unfortunately, delays at the local office are common.

Here's the reality: you're relying on Social Security to process your Medicare enrollment. If you're already receiving Social Security benefits, your Medicare enrollment may happen automatically. But if you're not, you'll need to apply yourself—and that process can take several weeks.

That's why it's critical to start three months before your 65th birthday. Giving yourself that buffer ensures you have time to get your Medicare Claim Number, review your coverage options, and enroll without rushing. Don't leave it to chance—give yourself the time you need.

THE MOST COMMON MISTAKE — CONFUSING ENROLLMENT PERIODS

One of the most common mistakes people make is assuming they can only make Medicare changes between October 15 and December 7, or the Annual Enrollment Period (AEP). This assumption often comes from years of experience with employer-sponsored group insurance, where open enrollment typically happens in November. It's understandable—after all, that's when you've been conditioned to make changes to your health benefits.

But here's the key difference: Medicare doesn't work like your old group plan. When you turn 65, you're granted a personal enrollment window that has nothing to do with the fall AEP. You don't have to wait until October to drop your employer coverage or enroll in Medicare. In fact, waiting could cost you access to better coverage or even cause a gap in benefits.

Your Turning 65 window is unique—and it only happens once. This is when you can make the most impactful decisions, including choosing a Medicare Supplement with no medical underwriting. Treat this time as a standalone opportunity, not something tied to the calendar year. Don't let the habits of your working years steer you wrong—Medicare has its own timeline, and it starts with you.

WHY THIS PERIOD IS SO VALUABLE — GUARANTEED ISSUE RIGHTS

What makes your Turning 65 Open Enrollment window so valuable? In short, it's your guaranteed ticket to the best coverage Medicare has to offer—without the usual hurdles. During this time, you're eligible to enroll in a Medicare Supplement plan (also known as Medigap) with no medical questions, no underwriting, and no chance of being denied—no matter your current health status.

Even if you're in the middle of ongoing treatments, recovering from surgery, or managing a chronic condition, you can still get in. That kind of access is rare in the insurance world. As one agent put it, "This is one of the few things the government got right."

Medicare Supplement plans are often called the Cadillac option because of their comprehensive coverage and predictable out-of-pocket costs. They give you the freedom to see any doctor who accepts Medicare and help protect you from large, unexpected bills.

But here's the catch—you only get this level of protection without underwriting during your personal Open Enrollment. Once this window closes, applying for a Supplement plan means going through health screening and approval. For full details on how these plans work, refer to Chapter 6: Medicare Supplement Plans.

WHAT HAPPENS IF YOU WAIT?

Many people don't realize that if you miss your Turning 65 Open Enrollment window and try to enroll in a Medicare Supplement (Medigap) plan later, the rules change dramatically. Outside of your initial enrollment period, these plans are no longer guaranteed issue—which means you'll be subject to full medical underwriting.

That includes a detailed health questionnaire and often

a phone interview to assess your current and past medical conditions. If you've developed any serious health issues since turning 65, you may be denied coverage entirely. Now, if you're healthy, you might still qualify. In fact, it's not uncommon for people in their 70s to switch to a new Medigap company to save money. But it only works if they're in good shape and can pass underwriting.

The safest and smartest approach? Lock in your coverage during your Turning 65 window, when the doors are wide open, and no one is asking questions about your health. If you want top-tier, hassle-free coverage that travels with you and gives you peace of mind, don't delay. This opportunity won't come around again.

WHAT ABOUT MEDICARE ADVANTAGE?

You may have heard of Medicare Advantage—also known as Part C—and wondered how it fits into the Open Enrollment picture. The great news is that Medicare Advantage plans never require medical underwriting. Whether you're turning 65 or switching plans later, there are no health questions, ever.

You can enroll in Medicare Advantage during your Turning 65 Open Enrollment period or the Annual Enrollment Period (AEP) between October 15 and December 7. That flexibility makes Advantage plans appealing, especially for those who may have missed their Medigap window or want an all-in-one plan that includes drug coverage and extra perks.

But it's important to understand that Medicare Advantage and Medicare Supplement are two very different types of coverage. Advantage plans operate within networks—often requiring you to see in-network doctors, get referrals, and follow plan rules. In contrast, a Medicare Supplement works alongside Original Medicare and typically allows access to any doctor nationwide who accepts Medicare.

Here's the key distinction: Medicare Supplement is only guaranteed issue during your Open Enrollment or delayed Part B enrollment. If you're healthy and prefer structured, network-based care, Advantage may work. But for broader access and fewer out-of-pocket surprises, Supplement still stands apart.

THE SECOND OPEN ENROLLMENT WINDOW — DELAYED PART B ENROLLMENT

If you're continuing to work past age 65 and staying on your employer's health plan, you might choose to delay your enrollment in Medicare Part B. That's completely allowed—and when you finally retire and enroll in Part B for the first time, you're given a second Open Enrollment window.

This window offers the same key benefit as your Turning 65 period: you can enroll in either a Medicare Supplement (Medigap) or a Medicare Advantage plan with no medical questions asked. No underwriting. No health screening. No chance of being denied due to pre-existing conditions.

But the timing is critical. From the effective date of your enrollment in Part B, you have 63 days to select a plan under these guaranteed issue rights. After that, if you try to apply for a Supplement plan, you'll face full underwriting just like anyone outside of these special periods.

This second window is a major opportunity—especially for those retiring later in life or transitioning off group insurance. If this applies to you, don't let the clock run out. Take advantage of the chance to get top-tier coverage without hassle, and make sure your healthcare keeps pace with your next chapter.

RECAP — THE TWO OPEN ENROLLMENT PERIODS

Let's break it down one more time. When it comes to getting guaranteed Medicare coverage without medical underwriting, there are only two Open Enrollment windows that offer this opportunity:

1. Turning 65 and enrolling in both Medicare A & B

This is your first and most well-known window. As you approach your 65th birthday, you have a seven-month enrollment period to enroll in Medicare and choose the plan that best fits your needs. During this time, you can enroll in a Medicare Supplement (Medigap) or Medicare Advantage plan—with no health questions asked. It's your best shot at locking in the highest level of coverage with no barriers.

2. Delayed Medicare Part B enrollment after age 65

This second window applies to those who delayed Part B enrollment because they stayed on an employer health plan. When you retire and enroll in Part B for the first time, you trigger a 63-day window to sign up for Medigap or Advantage without medical underwriting.

Miss either of these, and the rules change. If you're outside these windows, underwriting kicks in, and your health history could limit your options.

FINAL THOUGHTS — TAKE CONTROL OF YOUR TIMELINE

Medicare isn't one-size-fits-all, and neither is the enrollment process. That's why it's so important to understand your personal timeline. Whether you're approaching 65 or planning to retire a few years later, the choices you make—and when you make them—can have a lasting impact on your healthcare and your wallet.

Missing the Open Enrollment window tied to your 65th birthday or a delayed Part B enrollment doesn't just mean a little extra paperwork. It can mean losing access to guaranteed Medicare Supplement coverage, facing medical underwriting, or settling for a plan that doesn't fit your needs.

The good news? You don't have to navigate this alone. Start planning early, ask questions, and don't hesitate to work with a local, trusted Medicare agent who will walk you through your options and help you make confident, informed decisions.

When you act within your enrollment window, you take advantage of a system designed—at least in this case—to protect you. Don't let confusion or procrastination close a door that's wide open today. Take control of your timeline now, and you'll thank yourself for years to come.

CHAPTER 10

Annual Enrollment and Other Election Periods

Turning 65 is a one-time milestone—but Annual Enrollment is a date you'll want to remember every year. Between October 15 and December 7, Medicare has its Annual Enrollment Period (AEP)—a chance for current Medicare members to review their plans, make changes, or switch coverage entirely. Unlike your Turning 65 window, which only happens once, AEP comes around like clockwork every fall.

You'll know it's here when your mailbox fills up, your phone starts ringing, and every other commercial on TV is talking about Medicare. It can feel like information overload—but it doesn't have to be.

This chapter is here to help you cut through the noise, understand what matters, and make smart, stress-free decisions about your coverage. Whether you're happy with your current plan or thinking of switching, knowing what to look for during AEP can help you avoid surprises—and keep your healthcare right where it should be: working for you.

WHAT ANNUAL ENROLLMENT IS—AND WHY IT MATTERS

Annual Enrollment—also known as the Annual Election Period (AEP)—is your once-a-year opportunity to take a close look at your Medicare coverage and make changes if needed. Whether you're enrolled in a Prescription Drug Plan (PDP) or a Medicare Advantage Plan (MAPD), this is the time to evaluate your current benefits, compare what else is available, and switch if another plan better fits your needs for the upcoming year.

Officially, AEP runs from October 15 to December 7, but many Medicare agents begin helping clients as early as October 7. That extended window gives you more time to review changes, ask questions, and avoid a last-minute scramble. Your current plan may have added new costs, dropped coverage for certain medications, or changed its provider network—all things that could impact your healthcare and budget.

If you're already on Medicare, this is your annual check-in. Plans change. Your health might change. AEP is your chance to make sure your coverage still fits your life.

UNDERSTANDING THE ANNUAL NOTICE OF CHANGE (ANOC)

Every fall, around October 1, you'll receive a key piece of mail from your current Medicare plan—it's called the Annual Notice of Change (ANOC). Don't toss this one aside with the junk mail. It's one of the most important documents you'll get all year when it comes to your healthcare coverage.

The ANOC outlines all the changes coming to your plan for the next calendar year. That includes adjustments to your prescription drug coverage (like medications being dropped or moved to a higher tier), increases to copays and deductibles, and updates to your provider or hospital network. In some cases, benefits may improve—but often, you'll find out where your plan might fall short next year.

This is your first and best chance to decide if you're still in the right plan—or if it's time to shop around. Even if you've been happy with your coverage, the ANOC may reveal changes that could affect your costs or access to care.

Before you even start looking at other plans during Annual Enrollment, read through this notice carefully. It helps you make an informed decision—and ensures you're not caught off guard by surprises in January when your new plan year begins.

WHAT TO REVIEW WHEN COMPARING MEDICARE ADVANTAGE PLANS

When it comes time to compare Medicare Advantage Plans, there are five key areas you'll want to focus on. Even if you've been on the same plan for years—or if it still goes by the same name—don't assume the benefits are the same. Plans can (and often do) change every year. Here's what to look for:

1. **Provider Network:** This is where it all starts. Are your primary care doctor, specialists, and preferred providers still in the network? If they're not, you could be facing higher costs—or needing to switch doctors altogether.
2. **Medications:** Check to see if your prescriptions are still covered. Even small changes in the drug formulary or tier placement can have a big impact on your monthly costs. Your medication list should match the plan's drug list.
3. **Hospitals:** Make sure your local or preferred hospital is still in-network. If something unexpected happens, you want access to the care facilities you trust.
4. **Copays & Deductibles:** Look at key services like specialist visits, MRIs, labs, and hospital stays. Small changes may add up, especially if you have regular appointments or ongoing care.

5. **Maximum Out-of-Pocket (MOOP):** This is the absolute most you'll pay in one year for covered services. Some plans are increasing their MOOP significantly, so don't skip over this detail—especially if you have a condition that may require extensive treatment.

To make sense of it all, sit down with a licensed Medicare agent who understands your local options and can help you compare plans side-by-side.

YOUR AGENT'S ROLE DURING AEP

A trusted, local Medicare agent can make all the difference during Annual Enrollment. With dozens of plans available—and changes happening every year—it's easy to feel overwhelmed trying to sort through it all on your own. That's where a knowledgeable agent steps in.

Your agent knows what's changing in your specific county—from doctors joining or leaving plan networks to shifts in drug coverage to new plans being introduced. They can compare multiple plans side-by-side based on your doctors, prescriptions, preferred hospitals, and budget. Instead of guessing, you get a clear picture of which plan truly fits your needs.

One of the biggest perks? Their help is free to you. Medicare agents are paid by insurance companies, not by the customer. So there's no extra cost for their time or expertise—and no pressure to enroll in a plan that isn't right for you.

Working with an agent doesn't lock you into anything. It simply gives you an advocate—someone who can spot red flags, answer your questions, and help you make confident, informed decisions. If you're unsure about your current plan or just want to be sure you're getting the most out of your benefits, a good agent is a valuable ally.

WHAT IF YOUR PLAN GETS DISCONTINUED?

If you receive a Notice of Discontinuation in the mail, don't panic—it just means your current Medicare Advantage or Prescription Drug Plan won't be offered next year. While this might feel unsettling, the good news is you're not losing Medicare itself. However, you do need to take action before December 7 to make sure you're covered by a plan that fits your needs for the coming year.

When a plan is discontinued, you'll typically receive this notice in the fall, giving you time to shop for other options during the Annual Enrollment Period (AEP). If you don't make a new selection, Medicare may automatically enroll you in a similar plan offered by the same insurance company. But "similar" doesn't always mean "suitable."

Auto-enrollment might place you in a plan with a different network, new copays, or coverage gaps that weren't part of your original plan. That's why it's so important to review your options carefully—and ideally, sit down with a Medicare agent who can help you understand the changes.

If you've received a discontinuation letter, take it as a prompt to review your needs and make a proactive choice. With the right plan in place, you can head into the new year with peace of mind.

OPEN ENROLLMENT PERIOD (OEP) — THE QUIET BACKUP PLAN

The Open Enrollment Period (OEP) runs from January 1 to March 31 and often flies under the radar—but it's a valuable backup window for those enrolled in a Medicare Advantage Plan (MAPD). Not to be confused with turning 65. If you made a plan change during Annual Enrollment and now realize it's not working out, OEP gives you a one-time chance to make a switch.

During this time, you can:

- Switch from one Medicare Advantage plan to another, or
- Get rid of your Medicare Advantage plan and return to Original Medicare—and if you choose to, add a stand-alone Prescription Drug Plan (PDP)

It's important to know that OEP only applies to those already enrolled in a Medicare Advantage plan as of January 1. If you're on Original Medicare with or without a Medigap plan, or if you missed Annual Enrollment entirely, this window does not apply to you.

This period is especially helpful for those who quickly discover that their new plan isn't what they expected—whether it's a network issue, higher-than-anticipated costs, or coverage that just doesn't fit your health needs.

If you're unhappy with your Medicare Advantage plan early in the year, OEP is your opportunity to course-correct—but remember, you only get one chance, so make it count.

SPECIAL ENROLLMENT PERIODS (SEPS) — LIFE HAPPENS, AND MEDICARE KNOWS IT

A Special Enrollment Period (SEP) is Medicare's way of saying, "We get it—life happens." These flexible enrollment windows are triggered by specific life events that can affect your healthcare coverage. If you qualify for a SEP, you may enroll in or switch your Medicare Advantage or Prescription Drug Plan apart from the usual enrollment periods.

Some of the most common SEP triggers include:

- Moving to a new county or state where your current plan isn't offered
- Losing employer or union coverage, such as retiring after 65
- Becoming newly eligible for Medicaid or getting Extra Help

- Being affected by a natural disaster like a hurricane, flood, or wildfire
- Leaving incarceration and reentering the healthcare system
- Missing your Initial Enrollment Period (IEP) due to special circumstances

SEPs also apply to those who are new to Medicare and may have missed their IEP due to things like delayed retirement or unexpected life events.

One important note: SEPs are time-sensitive. Most give you a 60-day window from the date of the qualifying event to make a change. Miss that window, and you may have to wait until the next Annual Enrollment Period.

If something big in your life has changed, don't wait—talk to a Medicare agent to see if you qualify for a SEP and what options are available to you.

HOW TO KNOW WHICH PERIOD APPLIES TO YOU

With all the different enrollment windows, it's easy to feel unsure about which one applies to you—but it doesn't have to be confusing. Here's a simple way to figure it out:

- If you're already on Medicare and happy with your current plan, you still need to check for changes each fall during the Annual Enrollment Period. Your

plan might look the same on the surface but come with new costs, different coverage, or fewer benefits next year.
- If you just turned 65 or are retiring soon, your situation is different. Go back to Chapter 9 for everything you need to know about your Initial Enrollment Period—your personal, one-time window to get Medicare started the right way.
- If something major in your life has changed, like a move, job loss, or change in Medicaid status, don't guess—call a Medicare agent and ask if it qualifies you for a Special Enrollment Period (SEP).

Remember, the timeline you're in determines your options—including whether or not you'll need to go through medical underwriting for a Medicare Supplement plan. Knowing where you stand can help you make informed decisions and avoid missing out on those valuable coverage opportunities.

FINAL THOUGHTS — KNOW YOUR WINDOWS, PROTECT YOUR PEACE OF MIND

Medicare isn't something you set once and forget—plans evolve every year, and staying informed helps protect both your health and your wallet. Make it a habit to mark your calendar every fall and review any updates to your current coverage. Even small changes can have a big impact.

If all the options feel overwhelming, remember—you don't have to do this alone. A local Medicare agent can walk you through your choices, answer your questions, then help you make confident decisions. Knowing your enrollment windows—and using them wisely—brings peace of mind you can carry into every new year.

EPILOGUE

By now, you've hopefully gained a clearer understanding of what Medicare is, how it works, and how to make informed choices that fit your life—not someone else's. If your head is still spinning a little, that's okay. This is a big transition, and it's perfectly normal to have more questions as you move forward. Just take a deep breath. You're not behind, and you're not alone.

I've spent the past two decades helping people walk through this exact process, and if there's one thing I've learned, it's this: clarity comes with time, and peace comes with a plan.

So, what should you do next?

First, give yourself plenty of time. The earlier you start learning and preparing, the smoother this process will be. Don't wait until the last minute to begin exploring your options—even if you're still working and planning to delay enrollment. Understanding what's required now can save you headaches (and penalties) down the road.

Second, create a plan. Even if your plan is to delay Medicare for now, write it down. Know your deadlines. Stay organized. Think of this the way you might approach a big trip—you wouldn't wait until the night before to pack your bags or book your flight. Treat your Medicare enrollment with the same care and attention.

Finally, don't be afraid to ask for help. If you're not sure where to begin, talk to a licensed local agent. Someone who knows your state, your region, and your available carriers will be able to offer personalized help that an 800 number or website simply can't. Ask friends or neighbors for referrals—they're often the best source of trusted connections.

And remember: you can always reach out to us at **questions@christineames.com**. Whether you're just getting started or facing a tricky situation, our staff is here to help—or point you toward someone who can.

You deserve to feel confident in this next chapter. Medicare doesn't have to be a mystery. With the right tools, the right information, and a little guidance, you can move forward with clarity and confidence.

You've got this—and we've got your back.

– Christine Ames

www.ingramcontent.com/pod-product-compliance
Lightning Source LLC
Chambersburg PA
CBHW032051150426
43194CB00006B/490